MAKING IT IN ADVERTISING

Also by Leonard Mogel

Making It in the Media Professions

Making It in Public Relations

*The Magazine: Everything You Need to Know to Make It
in the Magazine Business*

MAKING IT IN

Advertising

AN INSIDER'S GUIDE TO
CAREER OPPORTUNITIES

Leonard Mogel

COLLIER BOOKS
MACMILLAN PUBLISHING COMPANY
NEW YORK

MAXWELL MACMILLAN CANADA
TORONTO

MAXWELL MACMILLAN INTERNATIONAL
NEW YORK   OXFORD   SINGAPORE   SYDNEY

Copyright © 1993 by Leonard Mogel

Collier Books
Macmillan Publishing Company
866 Third Avenue
New York, NY 10022

Maxwell Macmillan Canada, Inc.
1200 Eglinton Avenue East
Suite 200
Don Mills, Ontario M3C 3N1

Macmillan Publishing Company is part of the Maxwell Communication Group of Companies.

LIBRARY OF CONGRESS CATALOGING-IN-PUBLICATION DATA
Mogel, Leonard.
Making it in advertising: An insider's guide to career opportunities / Leonard Mogel.—1st Collier Books ed.
p.   cm.
Includes bibliographical references and index.
ISBN 0-02-034552-6
1. Advertising—United States.   2. Advertising—Vocational guidance—United States   3. Advertising agencies—United States.   I. Title.
HF5813.U6M57   1993
659.1'0973—dc20   92-32051
CIP

Macmillan books are available at special discounts for bulk purchases for sales promotions, premiums, fund-raising, or educational use. For details, contact:

Special Sales Director
Macmillan Publishing Company
866 Third Avenue
New York, NY 10022

First Collier Books Edition 1993

10 9 8 7 6 5 4 3 2 1

Printed in the United States of America

*To the new people in my life, Emma Charlotte Tolkin
and Jeremy Ethan Pitts.*

CONTENTS

PART III   ADVERTISING OUTSIDE THE AGENCY WORLD

PART IV   PURSUING A CAREER IN ADVERTISING

**PART V   FROM THE HORSE'S MOUTH: INTERVIEWS
WITH ADVERTISING PROS**

ACKNOWLEDGMENTS

Appreciation goes to my wife and best friend, Ann Mogel. Her contribution went beyond any words I can say.

My sincere thanks goes to my editor, Natalie Chapman, for her professional excellence, guidance, and intelligent advice. She brought the keenest of critical eyes to bear on the book. Thanks, too, to Nancy Cooperman for her cheerful cooperation, and to copy editor Frank Lavena.

I wish to thank all the people who enhanced this book by agreeing to be interviewed: Bill Pitts, Dick Low, Martha Pellington, Robin Cooper, Michelle Kastula-Green, Debra Weekley, and Roger Bumstead.

I may miss a few names, but my sincere appreciation for splendid cooperation goes to Joyce Harrington of the American Association of Advertising Agencies; Jack Thomas of *ADWEEK;* Renee Paley of the Association of National Advertisers; Chuck Jones of Jones-Lundin Associates; John Veronis and John Suhler of Veronis, Suhler and Associates; Bill Holiber of Cowles Business Media; *The Standard*

Directory of Advertising Agencies and *The Standard Advertising Register;* Phil Suarez of Giraldi/Suarez Productions; the American Advertising Federation; Kathy Cripps of Nelson Communications; Jerome Pickholz and Ray Roel of Ogilvy & Mather Direct; the School of Visual Arts; the Advertising Research Foundation; Patricia Ransom of Lintas: New York; Frederick Lamparter of Ogilvy & Mather Worldwide; Ella Strubel of Leo Burnett Company; Robert Giacomino of Grey Advertising; Susan Irwin of McCann-Erickson Worldwide; James Porcarelli of D'Arcy Masius Benton & Bowles; and Aviva Ebstein of Young and Rubicam.

A special thanks to the Thousand Oaks Library for the use of their excellent facilities.

PART I

Introduction to Advertising

CHAPTER 1

A Short History of Advertising

What is advertising? Advertising takes many forms:

It is the $850,000 per thirty-second television commercial on the Super Bowl broadcast.

It is the four-inch ad for Jiffy Lube in your local newspaper.

It is the double-page full-color ad for a new Estée Lauder fragrance in *Vogue*.

It is also the display card in a department store for that same fragrance.

Advertising is the streamer for a sunscreen product on a small plane flying over a beach.

Those pesky, unsolicited mailings we receive daily on behalf of charities, magazine subscriptions, and insurance plans are advertising.

Way back, when a man would walk the city street with a sack on his back, chanting to the housewives, "I cash clothes, I cash clothes," that was a primitive form of advertising.

One writer defined advertising very simply: "Advertising is messages, telling people something." Another more formal definition calls advertising "the act or practice of calling public attention to one's product or service, need, etc., by paid announcements in newspapers, magazines, radio, TV, or on billboards to get more customers." We will broaden these definitions by describing the uses and practices of the dynamic profession of advertising. But first let us discuss the history of advertising.

Personal selling, or word-of-mouth advertising, probably goes back to prehistoric times. It was used to sell something one no longer needed or wanted to exchange for something else.

An early form of advertising, "criers," originated in Babylonia in 3000 B.C. People would take to the streets carrying their merchandise and shouting their wares. Later, merchants would hire criers with good loud voices to sell for them.

The Babylonians even used outdoor advertising. Because few persons could read in those days, a sign was placed outside an establishment with a crude illustration of the vendor's product.

The earliest written advertisement is some three thousand years old—a sheet of papyrus bearing the notice of a runaway slave and a reward for his return. It was found in the ruins of Thebes, in Egypt, and is preserved in the British Museum.

The ancient Egyptians used an early form of what we today refer to as saturation advertising. They carved advertising messages on stone slabs and placed them along the main roads for people to see. The same message was repeated on many tablets for emphasis, a forerunner of the Burma Shave signs that dotted the countryside fifty years ago.

During the Middle Ages, merchants were often afraid to let it be known that they had valuable goods for fear of being robbed. Where they felt safe, they used criers and signboards. In France, wine shops employed men who dispensed samples in the streets. In England, signboards became a part of the national tradition.

THE INVENTION OF PRINTING AND EARLY PUBLICATION ADVERTISING

Johannes Gutenberg's invention of movable type, around 1450, greatly increased the use of printed messages to sell merchandise and services. In 1480, William Caxton, England's first printer, posted a handbill on church doors advertising a book. Printed handbills and posters became common in the 1600s.

Advertising flourished with the introduction of the first English daily newspaper in 1702, the *London Daily Courant*. The noted essayist Joseph Addison was a contributor to the paper. An advertiser in the *Courant*, Dr. Chamberlen's Anodyne Necklace, was one of the first to use testimonials to draw attention to its trademark.

The first newspaper advertising in the United States was carried by the *Boston News-Letter* in 1704, but this was on a small scale, as the paper didn't reach a circulation of three hundred until forty years later. Ben Franklin's *General Magazine*, founded in 1741, carried paid advertising. Although England had the jump on the United States in advertising, by the early 1800s the United States had taken the lead and never relinquished it. The use of advertising, however, was very limited in publications until the 1850s, when printing developed rapidly and literacy increased among the general population.

After the Civil War, a tremendous industrial expansion enabled many manufacturers to mass-produce goods of uniform quality for the first time. The manufacturers realized that by the use of advertising they could reach a large number of people and persuade them to buy.

Along with growth in the production of goods and the need for manufacturers to advertise came an increase in the advertising vehicles themselves; that is, the newspapers and magazines where the advertising was placed. A key event was the 1849 invention of the rotary press, which produced newspapers far more speedily and efficiently than the original flatbed press. The manufacture of paper from wood pulp began in 1866, the linotype in 1884, and the halftone engraving in 1893.

THE ORIGIN OF ADVERTISING AGENCIES

The first advertising agencies began in the early 1800s, a period when newspapers proliferated. The operations of these newspapers depended then, as today, on advertising revenues.

In those days, sellers purchased space directly from the newspaper publishers. When this practice became unwieldy, the publishers hired salesmen to sell ad space. The salesmen acted as "brokers" for the space, purchasing it in blocks from the publishers at a discount and then selling it to the customers at full price. The broker's discount was usually 15 percent. The same commission structure and discount prevail today between advertising agencies and newspapers, magazines, and other print media where they place advertising for their client-advertisers.

Soon advertisers came to depend on the brokers to create their advertising, and the brokers began hiring specialists to write the ads. And that's how advertising agencies started.

The first U.S. agency was founded by Volney B. Palmer in Philadelphia in 1840. Ads of that period were filled with boastful claims for strange elixirs with amazing curative powers for dozens of diseases.

In the 1900–20 period, a new trend emerged in advertising—celebrity testimonials. The noted actress Ethel Barrymore praised petticoats; the great dancer Anna Pavlova pitched O'Sullivan's rubber heels; and another famous actress, Ina Claire, pushed hats. Once we were exposed to celebrity testimonials, we had them with us forever.

In the early 1900s, Cyrus H. K. Curtis founded the first big magazines (among them the *Saturday Evening Post*); they became important advertising media. Radio advertising got started in the early 1920s; television advertising, in the immediate post–World War II period. Modern advertising has been a part of our culture for a hundred years. Where would we be without it?

ADVERTISING TODAY

Advertising now encompasses television, radio, films, newspapers, and magazines—sight and sound, as well as print. Advertising familiarizes people with brand names, spreads news about product improvements, cooperates with a dealer's own promotions, helps close the sale, and reassures customers after they have bought the product. Unless advertising can attract, convince, and persuade, it is a complete waste.

Today the bulk of jobs in the advertising profession are found in the more than ten thousand advertising agencies that create and place advertising of every type in thousands of media sources. Most of the remaining jobs in advertising are found with the clients of these agencies—that is, the more than twenty thousand manufacturers, retailers, and organizations that hire their services and rely on these agencies to "sell" their product.

A third source of advertising jobs is with companies and organizations that produce their own advertising rather than hiring outside ad agencies.

We will discuss the three groups, describe the job functions and salaries of various advertising positions, look at the media (television, radio, newspapers, and magazines) where advertising is placed, profile the nation's largest advertisers and agencies, offer advice on career planning and preparation, and discuss trends in advertising today.

First, though, we'll take a look at what advertising encompasses—its components—and explore the complex world of the advertising agency.

CHAPTER 2

The Components of Advertising and Promotion

The business of advertising has three basic components: promotion, media advertising, and "other" advertising.

Promotion involves activities designed to implement the sales and advertising process. Coordinating participation in a telephone answering services trade show by a company such as AT&T is an example of promotion. Agencies may become involved in these activities, but more often they are the responsibility of the advertiser.

Media advertising is the placement of prepared advertisements in print and electronic media. An example would be AT&T's ad campaign in magazines and newspapers or their TV commercials promoting long-distance service. Most often, this advertising is the province of ad agencies, which prepare the ads or commercials, determine where they will be placed, and monitor their effectiveness.

"Other" advertising includes ancillary or peripheral sources of advertising, such as AT&T's direct-mail campaign to sell their services to businesses.

PROMOTION

Trade shows and exhibits

Point-of-purchase display

Premiums and incentives

Conventions and meetings

MEASURED MEDIA ADVERTISING

Television

Radio

Daily newspapers

Consumer magazines

Business magazines

OTHER ADVERTISING

Direct mail

Yellow pages

Weekly newspapers

Transit poster displays

Matchbooks

Outdoor

Here is a brief description of each component:

PROMOTION

Trade Shows and Exhibits

Trade shows are industry expositions of products and services by various manufacturers in a particular industry. Usually, trade shows are held in an exhibition hall, convention facility, or the like and are open to dealers in the industry, and sometimes to the public as well. When a tool manufacturer, such as Stanley Tools, has a booth at the National Hardware Show, they not only display their latest line of products and meet their dealers and wholesalers; they also monitor their competitors. Preparations for these events are carefully planned by a company's own advertising department and its agency.

Point-of-Purchase Display

A point-of-purchase (also called point-of-sale) display is designed for use at a retail outlet where an item can be purchased. Stanley Tools may first promote a new line of hand tools at the National Hardware Show. There they may take orders from retailers for a large display showing a handyman using the tools, for use in the retail store. They will also make available colorful "dumps," standing containers filled with various products, to be placed in home-improvement stores. The arrangement for signs and banners in the stores also falls in the point-of-purchase category. Often the manufacturer will be required to pay a special display allowance for this privilege. Designing these dumps is usually the province of the manufacturer and not its ad agency.

Premiums and Incentives

Premiums and incentives are prizes, bonuses, or awards given as an inducement to purchase products and enter competitions initiated by manufacturers and retailers.

When you have trouble lifting your Sunday newspaper, it's often because the classified-advertising sections, rotogravure inserts, and the hundreds of redemption discount coupons double the paper's bulk. Advertisers commit to redemption-coupon programs in a major way because they bring results. Customers already using the product are encouraged to keep buying it, and others are attracted to it because of the price incentive.

These redemption coupons are also offered in mailings. Most often, the mailing is done by one company with a multiproduct line (e.g., Procter & Gamble or General Foods). These mailings are very expensive, and their results are carefully monitored.

Conventions and Meetings

A convention brings together a large group of companies, dealers, or services within a similar industry or profession for discussion and action on particular matters of common concern. Almost every major industry has regional or national conventions. Professional organizations, such as the American Medical Association (AMA), also have conventions for large groups and hold seminars within these conventions for smaller subgroups. At such AMA conventions, pharmaceutical manufacturers maintain a very visible presence.

At these conventions, the host organization will arrange for the distribution of printed material and programs as well as speeches and visual presentations. If the convention is related to the sales function, the company's sales department will work closely with its advertising department and its outside ad agency to coordinate presentations.

The field of business meetings and conventions is so vast that there are about thirty-five magazines covering such activities. One is devoted solely to medical meetings.

The sales or marketing department of a company or organization works closely with both its own sales promotion and advertising staff and its agency in its presentations for these conventions and meetings.

MEASURED MEDIA ADVERTISING

Television

Television reaches 92 million American households. There are over a thousand commercial TV stations that sell advertising airtime. Advertisers spend more each year on TV advertising than on any other media category except newspaper advertising.

TV commercials run the gamut from an $850,000, thirty-second spot on a Super Bowl broadcast seen by 120 million viewers to $500 for a full-minute commercial for Pizza Hut on a local station. Airtime is bought on a "network" basis, which means that the same ad appears on all the stations of that network, or on a "spot" basis, meaning the commercial runs only in specific cities. TV commercials are created and planned by ad agencies.

Radio

Radio is the other broadcast medium. There are approximately 10,500 radio stations in the United States; they feed their airtime to a half billion radio sets. The total amount spent on radio advertising is only about 30 percent of that spent on TV advertising. Most radio commercials are bought locally, not nationally. The rates stations charge are also usually quite negotiable, which makes radio advertising attractive to large, aggressive advertisers and their agencies.

Daily Newspapers

There are about seventeen hundred daily newspapers in the United States, all of which accept advertising. Although there were more dailies in 1946 than there are today, daily newspapers are still the leading advertising medium in terms of spending—$32.8 billion spent in 1990, almost 15 percent more than the amount spent on all TV advertising. Like TV ads, print ads usually originate with advertising agencies, with the exception of large retailers and department stores that have in-house ad departments.

Consumer Magazines

Consumer magazines are weekly or monthly publications of general or specialized interest either sold or given free to the public. *Family Circle* and *Sports Illustrated* are examples. Consumer magazines derive most of their income from the sale of advertising, which is bought either nationally (to run in the entire circulation) or regionally. The automotive industry is the largest spender in consumer-magazine advertising, with expenditures of almost $1 billion a year, closely followed by toiletries and cosmetics advertisers.

Business Magazines

Business magazines, sometimes called "trade" magazines, deal with the commercial and financial aspects of particular industries or businesses. *Modern Medicine, Travel Agent* magazine, and *Interior Design* are examples of business magazines. A pharmaceutical advertiser, such as Merck, will advertise a new arthritis drug in *Modern Medicine* to reach all its physician-subscribers. A tour operator specializing in Arizona tours will advertise in *Travel Agent* magazine to sell his services to travel agent–subscribers.

OTHER ADVERTISING

Direct Mail

Direct mail is advertising sent directly to the consumer through the mail. It is sometimes referred to as direct-response advertising. When you receive junk mail or even a solicitation from the Book-of-the-

Month Club, that's direct mail. Direct mail accounts for $24 billion in revenue in the United States. Direct mail is highly specialized, using modern computerized techniques. Specialists at ad agencies, and advertisers as well, perform the key functions of selecting and renting mailing lists, designing direct-mail brochures and fliers, and writing copy for the mailing pieces.

Yellow Pages

We've all "let our fingers do the walking," yet few of us know that the yellow pages are a major factor in spending by advertisers. Advertising in the yellow pages is very effective for local businesses and professionals. Moreover, a national advertiser will often subsidize the yellow pages advertising of its local dealers. For example, Carrier (air-conditioning) will have its logo and name in boldface in the yellow pages listing for Air Conditioning Contractors and Systems. Under this heading a dozen local Carrier contractors are listed. Carrier pays for most of the cost of this advertising.

Weekly Newspapers

There are about eight thousand weekly newspapers located primarily in small cities and towns. These papers sustain their operations on advertising revenues. The preparation of this advertising is a function of local advertising agencies and, in many cases, local advertisers. A department store in a city with a population of ten thousand will often prepare its ads in-house for insertion in weekly newspapers rather than hire an outside agency.

Transit Poster Displays

Posters displayed on buses and in subways are prepared by local ad agencies for local advertisers. In many cases, however, national advertisers, such as cigarette and beer companies, sponsor transit advertising.

Matchbooks

Matchbook advertising is used effectively by a limited number of advertisers.

Outdoor

Yes, there are still billboards marring the beauty of our highways, but more and more are subject to local and state controls. This form of advertising may be very effective for public-service messages. Although not a growth area, outdoor advertising still receives more than a billion dollars a year in ad spending.

Outdoor advertising is not confined to rural areas. It is very effective in New York's Times Square, Sunset Boulevard in Los Angeles, and Las Vegas, where movie advertising dominates the billboards.

Placing and preparing the advertising for all these components requires the services of specialists. They include people who do the market research; art directors and copywriters, who prepare the advertising; media planners, who are responsible for placing advertising where it will reach the right people at the right time in the right place and doing so cost-effectively; and the people who review the results.

BEYOND THE AGENCIES

Who does all this advertising? Mostly the ad agencies that represent advertisers. We discuss their complex role in Part II.

The advertisers are the companies whose products and services are promoted and marketed, usually through the agencies they contract to do the work. We describe their function in Part III. Often smaller organizations will create and place advertising directly, using in-house personnel and some outside contractors. We examine their activities as well in Part III.

Throughout the book we will analyze the operations of each of the three sources of advertising jobs, focusing on the job functions and careers available in each. We will discuss what people do and how they do it, how much they make, the degree of specialization each position entails, the difference between the business side and the creative side, the advantages and disadvantages of large and small agencies, the training, education, and characteristics you need to bring to particular jobs, and finally, how to get hired.

PART II

The World of
the Agency

CHAPTER 3

An Overview of the Advertising Agency

THE ADVERTISING-AGENCY BUSINESS

Before the emergence of the modern advertising agency, advertising was a do-it-yourself affair, with a few individuals in a small agency performing all the creative and business tasks. But that's not true today. There are just too many talents and skills that must be combined to make advertising succeed. In the past, an agency could individually farm out the various elements, such as copywriting and art direction, but today that is an impractical approach. The agency needs to control all its functions, and that is better accomplished under one roof.

Advertisers, or clients, as they are most often called in the world of advertising, come to the agencies for the implementation of their total marketing plan and the preparation of their advertising campaign. Why don't they do it themselves? Because they prefer to rely on a team of specialists in market research, advertising, and promotion.

An advertising agency is an organization of business and creative people dedicated to making advertising succeed. They are integrally involved in other aspects of marketing and selling, but their fundamental concern is the development of successful advertising.

There are just under 10,000 agencies in the United States employing a little more than 100,000 people, about half those employed in the entire advertising field. About one-third of the agencies are one-person operations, and another third employ two to five people. The other third range from small agencies to international giants employing thousands and billing more than $1 billion a year.

WHERE THEY ARE GEOGRAPHICALLY

New York City dominates the global ad-agency market. It is estimated that nine of ten world headquarters of agencies are in the Big Apple.

There are many reasons. New York has the largest concentration of creative talent, many client headquarters are there, and the media—broadcasting and publishing—are primarily directed from New York.

Chicago is second in total advertising billings; Los Angeles, third; Detroit (with its automotive business), fourth; and San Francisco, fifth. One should not assume that great advertising is not produced outside these cities. Award-winning campaigns have emanated from Minneapolis, Boston, Atlanta, and Dallas. These cities should not be overlooked in your career search.

Many agencies are generalists, yet some either specialize in advertising to a specific group, such as medical advertisers or the travel industry, or are geared to a particular type of advertising, such as direct mail, entertainment, or financial.

The Agencies' Global Village

Many American products are sold all over the world. Advertising is an increasingly international business and will become more so with the 1992 restructuring in Europe. Therefore, agencies with offices in foreign countries offer a distinct convenience to American companies selling their products abroad. When there are a hundred

McDonald's in the Russian republic, a Moscow branch office of their American agency will be able to service McDonald's there.

The challenge for multinational agencies is in complying with various international and national regulations and ad restrictions as well as the demands of important groups such as the European Economic Community. These agencies must also be concerned with national restrictions on health claims in food advertising and regulations on alcohol, pharmaceutical, and financial advertising.

THE ROLE OF THE AAAA

To maintain standards of conduct and competency, "the four A's," or the American Association of Advertising Agencies (AAAA), was formed in 1917. Membership is by application: An applicant's references and balance sheet are reviewed, and the applicant is then investigated and voted on by the 4A board. Member agencies handle some 70–75 percent of all the agency business in the United States.

There are more than seven hundred 4A member agencies operating more than twenty-one hundred offices in some three hundred cities in nearly every state (and in a hundred cities in other countries). They're big and small. *The Standard Directory of Advertising Agencies* (known as the Agency Red Book) lists all the agencies alphabetically and geographically and states their 4A affiliation, if any.

A basic qualification for 4A membership is that the agency be an *independent* business organization; that is, a 4A agency must be free from control to any degree by an advertiser, and it cannot be owned by an advertising medium or supplier. This requirement is based on the premise that only an independent agency can provide the unbiased and objective counsel that the advertiser needs.

The agency must also show that it is ethically operated and that it has character, ability, and financial capacity, among other criteria.

As the parent organization for so many agencies, the 4A's is concerned with many programs to strengthen advertising. One principal activity is the 4A Creative Code, which seeks to monitor false or misleading advertising, unfair price comparisons, unwarranted claims, and advertising that may run afoul of government agencies.

The 4A's are also sponsors of the Advertising Research Foundation (ARF) and the Advertising Educational Foundation, which gives grants to academics to foster research on how advertising works. For instance, a recent study, "Consumer Attitudes Toward Advertising," was separately funded by the 4A's at the Harvard Graduate School of Business Administration.

One important booklet from the 4A's is its "Guide to Careers in Advertising," which is given wide distribution through college placement offices and guidance counselors. The association also produces a series of excellent booklets for agency people to understand each other's functions. One such booklet is "What Every Account Executive Should Know About the Creative Function."

CHAPTER 4

Structure and Function
of an Agency

A n advertising agency performs the following basic functions for a client:

Market Research

The agency studies the client's product or service, compares it with the competition's, and checks its pricing, its packaging, its ranking in the marketplace, and the perceptions consumers hold about it and the competitor's products. The agency also analyzes the competitive advertising.

The agency makes a careful study of the present and potential market for the product or service. The study identifies the kinds of people who can use the product, their demographics (social and economic characteristics, such as sex, age, size of family, education, and income levels), and where they live. The agency also studies the seasonal and geographic factors affecting the product or service and the effect of trade and economic conditions on the business.

The research is obtained from many sources, such as interviews, field studies, trade associations, and so forth.

The agency puts into use its knowledge of how to get the product profitably to the point of sale—the store, the auto showroom, the bank, etc. It determines who are the best wholesalers, jobbers, retail stores, and chains for the client's product. Agency people constantly visit and study these outlets as well as interview consumers in their homes about their preferences and general buying habits.

Formulating a Plan

As we have already seen, an advertiser can spend money in many different places. The agency must understand all these media and their potential use. It must identify the best customers and then propose the media that will get the message to the buyer at the lowest effective cost. Media selection and evaluation are the most exacting arts of the agency business.

We now reach a key stage known as formulating the *plan*. In doing so, the agency makes its recommendations based on the following:

- market or markets to be reached
- possible changes in the distribution of the product
- pricing to the consumer, retailer, and wholesaler
- media channels to be employed—TV, radio, magazines, news-papers, outdoor advertising—that will carry the message to the consumer and the retailer and wholesaler
- copy and creative thrust to be used in each media channel
- merchandising factors (salespeople, dealers, distributors) to be contacted and brought into the effort
- the amount of money to be spent in each media channel

Execution of the Plan

Once the client has approved the overall budget and plan, the agency's creative people take over from the media and research staff. It is their job to put the advertising message into words and pictures.

Writers skilled in the use of words and the motivations that impel consumers start by writing copy. Art directors and their staff, working with copywriters, visually implement the writers' efforts.

For print ads, layouts are made. These are designed by art directors, who also specify typefaces. Assistants then make the mechanical pasteups of these pages. The final rendering of the art is usually done by free-lancers outside the agency.

For TV commercials, frame-by-frame "storyboards" (cartoonlike representations of the action) are produced by writers, art directors, and producers.

For TV and radio ads, the agency usually buys individual commercial announcements rather than sole sponsorship of a program. The agency people are involved in every stage of the production of commercials, although the actual filming and taping are done by outside production companies. Keeping all these preparations and materials on schedule, to meet the production and media deadlines, is an agency function called "traffic control." It is traffic's responsibility to see that these radio and TV commercials are ready on time and that client and legal approvals have been obtained.

The Follow-up Stage:
Analyzing the Effectiveness of the Campaign

After an ad or commercial is run, the agency verifies its appearance and performance. If a magazine ad is printed poorly, it is the agency's job to request a rerun. If a TV commercial doesn't run as scheduled, the agency must be aware of it and request new showings.

The agency receives bills from its suppliers—TV production houses, photographers, typesetters—and then bills the client. The agency will adopt some formula for services; that is, they will charge the client cost plus a percentage for the agency's profit. In the case of ads in magazines and newspapers, or TV and radio commercials, the agency bills the advertiser for the full amount of the space and time; in turn, the media allow commissions to advertising agencies. This has been a traditional practice since the earliest days of advertising. The rate of commission is usually 15 percent of the gross rate of the advertising space or time. However, the amount and terms of media commissions are matters of individual decision by media. These commissions are how the agency pays its salaries and overhead and earns a profit. So that the agency's and media's cash flow are in sync, the client generally pays the agency at or before the time payments are due the media. There are many variations on the commission system. Many agencies work with their clients on a "fee" basis. This may involve a minimum fee, against which media commissions are credited, or an overall fee agreed upon in advance.

STRUCTURE OF ADVERTISING AGENCIES

At the top level of a large ad agency is corporate management. These are the people who administer the agency's own business, report to the board of directors, work on attracting new business, and in general run the agency's show. At a smaller agency, this group is also involved in day-to-day account management and creative duties.

Under this corporate-management level, the agency is divided into two basic divisions: the business side, which is responsible for client relations, evaluating and purchasing media, research, traffic, and production; and the creative division, which actually creates the TV commercials, magazine and newspaper ads, and other elements of the client's campaign.

The larger the agency, the more people are employed in each of these three areas and the greater is the degree of specialization within each area. While a small agency may consist of a manager, an account executive, and an artist/copywriter, big agencies can have fifty to one hundred people working on each major account.

In a small, regional ad agency with eight or nine people and a half-dozen local accounts, the entire staff may share the account-management, media-selection, and creative functions of all the agency's clients. In a large agency the "group" system is employed. One group of people handles the contact, planning, and creative work for one or more clients; similar groups handle other accounts. Usually, all groups use a centralized media department. A group serving a very large account may have as many as thirty or forty people.

In the next chapter we'll give detailed descriptions of every job. Here we'll go into the general functions of each division in a medium-to-large-size agency.

The Business Side

The business side of an ad agency consists of three departments: account management, the media department, and the research department. An organizational chart might look like this:

ACCOUNT MANAGEMENT	MEDIA	RESEARCH
Management supervisor	Media supervisor	Research director
Account supervisor	Group media director	Senior research director
Account executive	Senior media buyer	Researcher
Assistant account executive	Media buyer	Research trainee
Account trainee	Assistant media buyer	
Account assistant	Media planner	
	Assistant media planner	

ACCOUNT MANAGEMENT. The primary responsibility of account management is to work directly with the client to define the marketing objective and come up with a plan to implement that program. Account management then conveys the client's objectives to the other departments of the agency so that the resources of the agency and the needs of the client connect.

MEDIA. The media department of an agency is responsible for placing advertising where it will reach the right people, at the right time, in the right place, and do so cost-effectively.

RESEARCH. The research department's basic function is to support the creative process by focusing on understanding consumer trends in a changing market. They accomplish this through interviews, focus groups, and market-research studies.

The Creative Side

After a plan is approved by the client, the agency's creative side takes over. It is their job to create the print ads and broadcast commercials that are part of the whole campaign. At each stage in this development everything must be approved by the client. It is a long, tedious, and exacting process.

The four main departments on the creative side are production and traffic, art, copywriting, and broadcast. An organizational chart might look like this:

ART	COPYWRITING
Art supervisor	Copy chief
Art group head	Copy group head
Senior art director	Senior writer
Art director	Copywriter
Assistant art director	Junior writer
Art assistant	Assistant copywriter
Illustrator	Copy trainee
Pasteup artist	

BROADCAST	PRODUCTION AND TRAFFIC
Producer	Print production manager
Associate producer	Traffic supervisor
Assistant producer	Traffic manager

Here is a brief description of the general function of each department:

ART. The art staff conceives the graphics for ads and commercials. Ideas are first developed through layouts and storyboards and ultimately realized through photography, illustrations, and videotapes that are used for print and broadcast advertising.

COPYWRITING. The copy people deal with printed and spoken words, crafting them around ideas so that they work as effective advertising. In many agencies they are as revered as superstars.

BROADCAST. The broadcast group at an agency is responsible for the creation and execution of radio and television commercials. Although agency people do not usually serve as directors of these commercials, they are totally involved in the taping and shooting.

PRODUCTION. On print advertising the production staff works with the agency's art and creative people and outside suppliers such as typographers and color separators. On radio and television commercials the production staff works with its own and outside producers to create the final versions of the advertising.

TRAFFIC. Traffic staff directs the flow of ads and commercials through the agency. This work also includes client approvals. Finally, they see to it that the whole job arrives at the publication or the broadcast station on time.

CHAPTER 5

Jobs in an Advertising Agency

The jobs described in this chapter are typically found in a medium-to-large-sized agency employing at least 350 people. Following are the major jobs in these agencies, their functions, the qualifications needed for each job, and the usual salary range as of 1992.

One must realize that salaries vary according to the size of the agency, its location, its profitability, and the individual's length of service. Also, bonuses and other perks are a consideration in one's total compensation.

The mix of personnel at a medium-to-large agency is as follows:

	PERCENT
Account management	25
Creative	25
Media	15
Production	10
Corporate management, accounting, and other support services	25

THE BUSINESS DEPARTMENT: ACCOUNT MANAGEMENT

Management Supervisor

JOB DESCRIPTION. This top-management executive is responsible for the administration of one or more major accounts at an agency. He or she is the agency's link with the client's highest-ranking advertising and marketing executives. He or she oversees the work of account executives, assistant account executives, and the entire account-management team. At many agencies the management supervisor will also try to generate new business by meeting with prospective clients and pitching the agency's services, sometimes with sample campaign ideas.

QUALIFICATIONS. The management supervisor must be experienced in marketing techniques, campaign planning, and the art of making successful contacts with clients. He or she must be a good business administrator. Most come up from the ranks of account executives and account supervisors. Usually at least five years' previous experience as an account executive is required.

CAREER PATH. Management supervisors usually hold the rank of senior vice president. They may be promoted to executive vice president, general manager, or president at an agency. Management supervisors usually start their careers as assistant account executives, then move on to account executive and account supervisor. The path takes a minimum of eight years.

SALARY RANGE. Top New York and Chicago agencies pay $100,000–$120,000 (with some salaries going up to $200,000). Smaller New York City agencies and most in other cities pay between $80,000 and $100,000, with some starting at $60,000.

Account Supervisor

JOB DESCRIPTION. On very large accounts the account supervisor acts as the principal liaison between the agency and the client and often is a corporate vice president. The account supervisor is charged with seeing that accounts under his or her responsibility generate a profit at the agency. In some agencies, he or she is in charge of three or four account executives.

QUALIFICATIONS. An account supervisor must be a strong, knowl-edgeable, and diplomatic leader. He or she must have a marketing and business background—an M.B.A. is a definite plus. According to Tony Hopp, executive vice president of Lintas: New York, "The account manager must be able to marshal, motivate, and deliver the resources of the agency at its optimum level to the client."

CAREER PATH. An account supervisor usually starts out as an assistant account executive and then moves up to account executive. The next step beyond supervisor is management supervisor. It takes a mini-mum of four to six years of account experience to rise to account supervisor. A possible job shift might see an account executive at a large agency move to account supervisor at a smaller agency, by-passing the time it might take to reach this level at a large agency.

SALARY RANGE. At top agencies the salary runs from $65,000 to $80,000. Smaller agencies pay $50,000–$65,000 for this job.

Account Executive

JOB DESCRIPTION. The account executive maintains day-to-day liaison with his or her counterpart at the client company, often the brand manager. He or she makes regular calls on the client to discuss strat-egy and media, review creative work, develop plans, and monitor the budget.

QUALIFICATIONS. The account executive must be a skillful organizer and analyzer and work well with the creative staff, the media de-partment, and the traffic/production staff.

CAREER PATH. Promotion is usually to account supervisor, which may also carry the title vice president. Account executives ordinarily start out as assistant account executives and require one and one-half to two years' experience before being promoted to this job.

SALARY RANGE. At top agencies an account executive will make $30,000–$40,000. Smaller agencies pay from $28,000 to $35,000 for this job.

Assistant Account Executive

JOB DESCRIPTION. In general the assistant account executive works with the account executive and assists in many areas, including traffic and production.

QUALIFICATIONS. A year or two in the advertising department of a manufacturer will help get the first job. Also, a first job in traffic or media research is often a practical stepping-stone to the account-management staff. Some very large agencies require either a B.S. in communications or an M.B.A. degree for this job.

CAREER PATH. The next step up is account executive. This is usually an entry-level job, although at some large agencies one must first serve as an account trainee or account assistant.

SALARY RANGE. Top agencies pay $20,000 and $23,000 for M.B.A.s. At smaller agencies, assistant account executives may start at $16,000–$18,000.

Account Trainee and Account Assistant

JOB DESCRIPTION. These jobs are below that of assistant account executive, whom they assist. The job exists mainly at large agencies.

QUALIFICATIONS. Often secretarial skills are required for this job classification. A college degree is a requirement.

CAREER PATH. One is promoted from this job to assistant account executive at a larger agency or to account executive if the move is made to a smaller agency. These are entry-level jobs.

SALARY RANGE. At large agencies, where most of these jobs are, the salary range is $15,000–$18,000.

THE BUSINESS SIDE: MEDIA DEPARTMENT

Innovative, analytical, energetic, adventuresome individuals who love to make a deal and enjoy interacting with people may have a basis for a career in media.

—Joel Kushins, senior vice president, media director, Bozell Inc.

The structure of media departments varies according to size and account assignments. At BBDO New York, for example, a fifty-person division develops media plans and supervises execution for twenty-seven clients and over eighty individual brands. This division of the agency's overall media department handles only print advertising and spends about $700 million a year.

On the next page is the organizational chart for a midsize New York agency that bills a little over $160 million a year.

Note that there is only one media buyer and an assistant compared to six media planners and three assistants. The agency's media department in this example spends about 64 percent of its billings on television, about 25 percent on print advertising, and the balance on radio and other media. The agency has one account over $20 million, with the average falling between $10 million and $19 million.

In this particular media department there is a Macintosh on every desk. There are no secretarial positions, all having been upgraded to media assistants.

Media Supervisor or Group Media Director

JOB DESCRIPTION. This individual is often the agency's top media executive, with the title senior vice president or vice president. He or she directs the formulation and execution of the advertiser's media plan and analyzes, recommends, and estimates costs of various media to fit the client's budget. The media supervisor must be completely familiar with the research data provided by the media, outside research organizations, and his or her own research department. A knowledge of statistics is essential. The media supervisor must be a good businessperson, a sharp negotiator, and a stickler for detail and accuracy.

CAREER PATH. From media supervisor one may rise to executive vice president, to group general manager, or at a smaller agency, to the rank of president. On the way up to this position, one progresses from media buyer, media planner, and senior media buyer.

SALARY RANGE. At a large agency the salary range is $75,000–$150,000. At smaller agencies, the range is $40,000–$75,000.

MEDIA DEPARTMENT ORGANIZATIONAL CHART

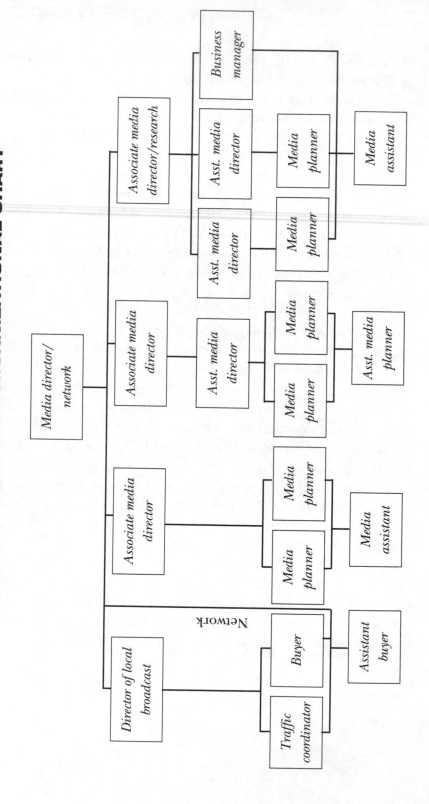

Senior Media Buyer

JOB DESCRIPTION. The senior media buyer spends the client's money according to an agreed plan. He or she consults with the various sales representatives of magazines, newspapers, radio, TV, and outdoor billboard advertising on rates, preferred positions (e.g., back cover of a magazine), special discounts, and so on.

QUALIFICATIONS. This job requires good analytic and organizational skills, plus a facility with statistics. The senior media buyer must have the ability to weigh competitive claims and negotiate the best deals. A degree in math and statistics is helpful preparation for this job.

CAREER PATH. The senior media buyer may first be promoted to media director, then media supervisor. On the way up, one would pass through the ranks of media trainee and media buyer. To move from entry level to senior media buyer takes three to four years.

SALARY RANGE. In large agencies the range is $35,000–$44,000; in small agencies, $30,000–$37,000.

Media Buyer

JOB DESCRIPTION. The media buyer implements the buying decisions of his or her superiors, the senior media buyer and media supervisor. Haggling and price negotiation are a part of the job.

QUALIFICATIONS. The media buyer must have complete familiarity with the media. Bargaining with media representatives requires shrewdness and a close working relationship with the salespeople. A degree in marketing, economics, English, or mathematics is valuable preparation for this job.

CAREER PATH. The next move up is senior media buyer or media director. One progresses to this position from assistant media buyer or assistant media planner. The path to this position from entry level usually takes two years.

SALARY RANGE. At large agencies media buyers earn from $25,000 to $29,000. At small agencies the range is $22,000–$26,000.

Assistant Media Buyer

JOB DESCRIPTION. The typical assistant media buyer reports directly to a media buyer and knows when and where space and time are available for purchase. The assistant media buyer also checks print ads and broadcast commercials to see that they are run as planned and at the agreed upon price; then calculates rates, usage, and budget; learns buying terminology and operating procedures; develops skills in negotiation and communication with media sales representatives; and becomes familiar with the media market.

QUALIFICATIONS. Successful candidates have strong general business skills, the ability to write and speak effectively, organizational skills, aptitude for working with numbers and statistics, and basic computer skills (e.g., spreadsheet software).

In addition, other important attributes are working well under pressure; maintaining priorities while handling a variety of tasks simultaneously; the ability and desire to interact with a wide range of personalities at the agency, at the client's business, and within the media industry; an understanding of sales and negotiation concepts; and a winning personal attitude. A bachelor's degree is an essential; a degree in advertising or marketing is an advantage.

CAREER PATH. One is promoted from this job to media buyer in one to one and a half years. The position is generally entry-level. Assistant media planners and buyers are not married to this specialty. Often people move to research or account management if they fit the personality requirement for this client-oriented function. Of course, moving to another agency's media department for more money is always a possibility.

SALARY RANGE. The general range for this position is $15,000–$20,000, perhaps a bit higher when one has an advanced degree, such as an M.B.A.

Media Planner

JOB DESCRIPTION. When a media planner is putting together the mix of print and broadcast advertising for a client-advertiser, he or she discusses with the client and other agency people the goals of the marketing strategy and the potential customer for the product or service. The planner must be aware of the kinds of media the target consumer might read, listen to, or watch. He or she compares the content, image, and format of each medium with the nature of the product or service, its image, and the goals of the advertising campaign.

QUALIFICATIONS. As with the media planner's counterpart, the media buyer, this individual must understand the demographics—age, income, education—concerning the media and its audience. The planner must also have complete familiarity with the client's product so that he or she may place the advertising in the best media for that product. The educational requirement is a degree in economics, business, or statistics.

CAREER PATH. Media planners move up the ladder to media director. One typically reaches this position from a job as assistant media planner or media assistant. As with media buyers, the path to this job takes about two years.

SALARY RANGE. At large agencies media planners earn from $25,000 to $29,000. At small agencies the range is $22,000–$26,000.

Assistant Media Planner

JOB DESCRIPTION. The typical assistant media planner reports to a media planner and gathers and studies information about people's viewing and reading habits; evaluates editorial content and programming of various media; learns all there is to know about the print and broadcast media; and becomes thoroughly familiar with media data banks and information sources.

QUALIFICATIONS. To accomplish these tasks requires the ability to find and analyze data, apply computer skills, ask innovative questions, and interpret or explain findings, with particular attention to the size of the audience reached and the characteristics of that audience. In short, a planner must know what information is important and where to find it. A bachelor's degree with a concentration in business, advertising, or communications is a prerequisite for this job.

CAREER PATH. One moves from this job to media planner in about one and one half years—and then to media director. The position is generally entry-level.

SALARY RANGE. The general range for this position is $15,000–$20,000; higher with an M.B.A.

Entry-level media-department jobs are generally low-salaried. However, there are advantages. For one, the media department, along with account management, hires the greatest number of entry-level candidates. It also offers an excellent learning opportunity. Pro-

in any job situation, comes with experience and talent.
ways room at the top, either at one's own agency or at
ice there, the salaries and perks make the wait worthwhile.

THE BUSINESS SIDE: RESEARCH

*Research is one of the most exciting areas in an advertising agency. You
are always working on new things and looking at new products.*

**—Bruce Childers, executive vice president,
marketing services, Meldrum & Fewsmith, Inc.**

Research Director

JOB DESCRIPTION. It is the job of the research director and his or her
staff to understand the wants, desires, thoughts, concerns, motivating
forces, and ideals of the consumers of the clients' products. The
research director supervises this function by conducting focus groups
or one-on-one interviews, testing people's reactions to new advertising, tracking sales volume, and studying business trends. He or she
may also specialize in specific areas of quantitative or qualitative research. The research director and staff work as advisers to the account, creative, and media people in the agency. At a large agency
this position is usually a senior vice president.

QUALIFICATIONS. In addition to a knowledge of all the creative and
business functions of the agency, the research director must understand the media and its audience characteristics. Many research directors at large agencies have master's- or Ph.D.-level training.

CAREER PATH. One achieves this post from agency experience as
researcher and senior researcher.

SALARY RANGE. At large agencies salaries range from $50,000 to
$72,000. At small agencies the job may be called senior researcher
or researcher, with a lower salary.

Senior Researcher or Researcher

JOB DESCRIPTION. In addition to pursuing many of the functions described for the job of research director, the senior researcher or researcher will oversee projects that are subcontracted to "out of house" research firms. A good example is a survey of shoppers of supermarkets. The agency researchers design the questionnaires and interpret results, but a private firm conducts the interviews and summarizes the data so that the researcher can write a report on the survey.

QUALIFICATIONS. Many employers are attracted to candidates whose coursework is related to research. Some academic disciplines fitting this category are sociology, psychology, marketing, economics, advertising, and mass communications.

CAREER PATH. The move upward leads to the job of research director or into general corporate management.

SALARY RANGE. Since these positions exist only at large agencies, accurate salary information is not available. The general range is probably $40,000–$55,000.

Research Trainee

JOB DESCRIPTION. This assistant reports to a researcher or senior researcher. Basic duties include compiling data from secondary resources, following the progress of research projects, evaluating basic consumer trends, and learning to analyze facts and numbers and interpreting and explaining what they really mean.

QUALIFICATIONS. Candidates must possess quantitative skills and the aptitude for analyzing and interpreting qualitative as well as quantitative data. A bachelor's degree in math and statistics is a minimum requirement, but many candidates have advanced degrees. Some agencies like to hire people who have had three or four years of full-time experience with an independent research firm or with an advertising research department.

CAREER PATH. This job leads to a supervisory position with the responsibility of managing research on individual accounts and overseeing the work of assistant researchers. The position is entry-level and exists primarily at the largest agencies or at advertising and marketing research firms.

SALARY RANGE. Since there are only a limited number of these jobs, it is difficult to set a salary range. Generally, these jobs receive the same salaries as other entry-level jobs at a large agency—higher when the candidate has an advanced degree.

THE CREATIVE SIDE

Creative Director

JOB DESCRIPTION. In the film industry, it is the director's vision and execution of that vision that make the picture a creative success or failure. In a similar sense, the creative director in an ad agency is the superstar of the agency business. At Young & Rubicam, one of the world's largest agencies, three creative directors share the title of vice chairman of the agency, two hold the rank of executive vice president, and eight are senior vice presidents.

The creative director is entrusted with creating the selling ideas and presenting these concepts to clients. The creative director is responsible for a client's total advertising program, including TV and radio commercials, print ads, and outdoor billboards. He or she directs the creative activities of the art directors, copywriters, producers, and other creative people. At large agencies the creative director or group creative director is responsible for a number of accounts. All the art and copy people on these accounts report to the creative director.

QUALIFICATIONS. It is not a requirement that creative directors have art and copywriting experience, but in practice one typically moves up from these ranks. What is singularly important is the creative director's talent and ability to motivate creative people. He or she must be diplomatic in relationships with the account-management people at the agency and the client as well.

CAREER PATH. Creative directors often move to the top of agencies or leave large agencies to form smaller ones. They reach the level of creative director from jobs as art director and copy chief. There is no single educational requirement for the job, but most creative directors are college graduates.

SALARY RANGE. At large agencies creative directors earn from $80,000 to $150,000 plus bonuses and perks. Even at smaller agencies, the job pays well, from $60,000 to $80,000.

THE CREATIVE SIDE: ART

Art Supervisor or Art Group Head

JOB DESCRIPTION. The art supervisor, also known as the art group head, supervises the work of art directors and assistants in preparing print ads and TV commercials. He or she also approves and directs all outside assignments.

QUALIFICATIONS. One need not be an artist or illustrator to rise to this rank at an agency. What is important is the ability to create effective visual images by marshaling the agency's art staff and outside individuals and services. Most people who reach this level have art-school degrees and special training in such areas as design, graphics, photography, and cinematography.

CAREER PATH. Promotion from this job leads to associate creative director or creative director. One reaches this level after at least five years of service as an assistant art director and then art director.

SALARY RANGE. The range is $50,000–$70,000 at large agencies and $40,000–$50,000 at smaller agencies.

Senior Art Director or Art Director

JOB DESCRIPTION. The title of senior art director is primarily used at large agencies. The art director creates visual images that are translated into TV commercials and print ads. In many agencies the art director is part of a creative team that also includes copywriters. The art director selects layout, type, art, and photos for print ads. He or she often draws storyboards for TV commercials and works closely with the TV producer. The art director is involved in every stage of an ad's development.

QUALIFICATIONS. The art director must have a fertile imagination, creativity, good judgment, a well-developed understanding of advertising, and the ability to communicate through visual images.

CAREER PATH. The path from art director leads upward to art group head and then, perhaps, creative director. One needs about four to five years' experience as an assistant art director to reach this level. Some have made the move from magazines to agencies.

SALARY RANGE. At large agencies the range is $40,000–$50,000; at smaller agencies the range is $35,000–$45,000.

Assistant Art Director or Art Assistant

JOB DESCRIPTION. This person performs many of the same functions as the art director. The assistant art director assists one or more art directors in preparing pasteups, rough lettering, and layouts for print ads and TV storyboards, developing visual concepts and designs, and overseeing photo sessions and the filming of TV commercials.

QUALIFICATIONS. Visual imagination and good basic drawing and design ability are important requisites. One may make the move to ad agencies from similar work at company advertising departments and commercial-art studios. Art-school training or art and advertising courses at college are clearly advantageous.

CAREER PATH. An assistant art director moves up the ladder at an agency to art director, then possibly to creative director. One pursuing this career path should definitely take desktop publishing courses at college or in college extension programs. This technology is now in broad use at agencies, magazines, and in other industries. Whole pages and ads are "drawn" and "laid out" on the computer monitor. With some experience at an agency, an assistant art director can move in many different directions.

SALARY RANGE. At large agencies the range is $20,000–$30,000; at smaller ones it is $18,000–$24,000.

Illustrator

Most agencies use free-lance illustrators. In New York and other large cities, there are hundreds of talented people in this specialty. Large agencies, however, may have illustrators on staff for the convenience of rush presentations. Salary range for staff is $19,000–$28,000.

Pasteup Artist

This individual assembles all the elements of an ad—type, art, and photos—and mechanically places them on a board ready for the printing or reproduction process. Salary range is $16,000–$19,000. Free-lancers earn about $12 per hour.

THE CREATIVE SIDE: COPYWRITING

> *Treat each copywriter with deference: you may be working with the next messiah. The copywriter deals in printed and spoken words, fashioning them around an idea so as to make an advertisement read or speak properly. Good copywriters must always be conceptualizers before they are wordsmiths. Words themselves are simply scribble unless they serve to illuminate an idea.*

—Ad veteran Carl K. Hixon

Some of the most memorable of all advertising men—Leo Burnett, David Ogilvy, Bill Bernbach, and Ray Rubicam—were copywriters. They all went on to run large agencies. Today's copywriting giants are no less gifted. Star copywriters are the José Cansecos of the ad-agency business, banging out their word home runs.

Copy Chief and Copy Group Head

JOB DESCRIPTION. Words are the essence of the function of the copy chief (also known as the copy group head). The copy chief who can come up with a catchy phrase or slogan receives star treatment at the agency. He or she oversees the staff of copywriters in creating ads for print and broadcast.

QUALIFICATIONS. A prerequisite is long experience as a copywriter who can evaluate good copywriting and motivate a staff to produce it. The copy chief must be able to translate product and consumer research data into copy that will effectively trigger a response in the consumer.

CAREER PATH. Copy chiefs become creative directors. They start out as junior and senior writers and rise to this eminent position after at least five years of experience—less at a small agency.

SALARY RANGE. At large agencies the range is $48,000–$80,000 plus bonuses and perks. At smaller agencies it is $35,000–$48,000.

Senior Writer and Copywriter

JOB DESCRIPTION. The copywriter generates scripts for broadcast commercials and copy for print ads. The focus for all advertising often starts with the copywriter who evolves the campaign theme, although the advent of the art director/writer team has given equal status to the art side of creative development.

QUALIFICATIONS. The job requires strong writing and verbal skills. The copywriter must have the ability to create attention-getting themes and headlines and to write strong copy for both print and broadcast.

CAREER PATH. Success at this level leads to the job of copy chief. One needs at least three years as an assistant to become a copywriter. This experience may be accumulated outside an agency.

SALARY RANGE. At large agencies the range is $30,000–$40,000 (much more if you're a star); at smaller ones it is $28,000–$35,000.

Junior Writer, Assistant Copywriter, or Copy Trainee

JOB DESCRIPTION. As in most entry-level advertising jobs, junior writers are expected to work hard and prove their worth. He or she assists one or more copywriters in editing and proofreading ad copy, writing body copy for established print campaigns, and developing merchandising and sales-promotion materials. With proven ability and experience, assignments might include generating ideas for product names and writing dialogue for TV commercials and scripts for radio ads.

QUALIFICATIONS. A junior writer needs outstanding skills in writing and, as one source expressed it, must have a "love affair" with words and symbols and their use in communication. An interest in many subjects and a sense of curiosity are assets. One should also have some knowledge of marketing and how words and visuals have been used in advertising.

Although a bachelor's degree is not required, a combination of liberal arts and appropriate business courses provides a good educational base. It is important to supplement formal education with actual writing experience. There are more jobs with advertisers (including department stores), media, and trade associations than there are at ad agencies.

CAREER PATH. Promotion within an agency leads to the job of senior copywriter. Although this job is entry-level, writing for school and community publications offers good training.

THE CREATIVE SIDE: BROADCAST

Producer

JOB DESCRIPTION. The producer coordinates the many production details of the TV commercial. He or she prepares the budget and works closely with the copywriter and art director. The producer selects the director and production company best suited for the job, consults with the set designer, and works with the casting director and the sound and music specialists.

QUALIFICATIONS. A producer needs a solid grounding in film production. This may be achieved by work as an assistant at an outside film commercial studio or at the agency itself. Film school or film courses at college are excellent preparation for this career. At the giant Young & Rubicam agency, TV producers reach the rank of senior vice president.

CAREER PATH. The highest post at a large agency for this specialty is executive vice president, director TV production. Reaching the level of producer means at least five years of experience—starting out as a gofer and then working as an assistant producer.

SALARY RANGE. At large agencies, $40,000–$50,000. At smaller ones the job may not exist if the agency doesn't handle much TV. For those that do, the salary range is $30,000–$40,000.

Associate and Assistant Producer

JOB DESCRIPTION. The associate or assistant producer performs many of the same jobs as his or her boss but is more involved with details, such as the complex technical, legal, and cost factors of making TV and radio commercials.

QUALIFICATIONS. This job requires training similar to that of the producer. One needs to develop "people" skills and have a broad knowledge of the filmmaking process. It also helps to have a good business head, since the job of producer and assistant producer involves the spending of large sums of money. A bachelor's degree is not required but is helpful.

CAREER PATH. The next step up is producer. Getting to this level may involve work as a production assistant at an agency, film studio, or tape studio.

SALARY RANGE. The range is $24,000–$33,000.

THE CREATIVE SIDE: PRODUCTION

Broadcast Production Manager

JOB DESCRIPTION. The real nuts-and-bolts people in an agency are the production managers. The broadcast production manager works with the producer and his or her assistants in controlling the flow of material for TV and radio commercials. Most often this work is done by suppliers outside the agency structure. He or she also works with the "talent" (actors, singers, musicians, etc.).

QUALIFICATIONS. You would accumulate this varied experience with jobs at a production house or as an assistant at a large agency. Film and mass-communications courses at college are also helpful in landing a job.

CAREER PATH. At large agencies, you may move from jobs as broadcast production manager to producer and then to management rank. Inevitably you break into this field as a gofer and then assistant broadcast production manager.

SALARY RANGE. At large agencies the range is $32,000–$40,000. At smaller agencies it is $28,000–$33,000.

Print Production Manager

JOB DESCRIPTION. This individual supervises the production, printing, scheduling, and budgeting of all advertising, outdoor print, and print "collateral" (brochures, folders, letters, fliers, and the like).

QUALIFICATIONS. He or she must know all graphic arts and printing processes. Handling details is a major part of the job's responsibility. Good prior experience might be work at a printer or type house. College training in graphic arts is an advantage.

CAREER PATH. This job classification exists at most agencies. At large ones, a print producer and assistant report to the print production manager. Print production managers at large agencies may hold the rank of vice president and, in some cases, senior vice president.

SALARY RANGE. From $25,000 to $32,000.

THE CREATIVE SIDE: TRAFFIC

Traffic Supervisor or Traffic Manager

JOB DESCRIPTION. The traffic department follows an ad or commercial as it works itself through the agency. Traffic personnel make sure deadlines are met, revisions are made promptly and correctly, and approvals are obtained at each stage. They generally keep things flowing so that the whole job arrives at the publication or the broadcast station on time.

QUALIFICATIONS. People involved in traffic must be able to work under the constant pressure that an agency's fast pace produces. A college degree helps get that first job.

CAREER PATH. A move upward from here may lead into account management. One typically breaks into this field with a job as traffic assistant.

SALARY RANGE. At large agencies the salaries range from $28,000 to $35,000; at small agencies, from $22,000 to $30,000.

Each year *Advertising Age* publishes an agency salary survey of ad-agency positions. The results are compiled from agencies nation-wide. Here are some averages for 1992:

TITLE	AVERAGE SALARY
Creative director	$85,700
Chief copywriter	54,200
Art director	48,400
Senior account executive	59,300
Account executive	39,800
Media director	50,600

Note: These salaries do not include benefits, bonuses, or perks.

Source: *Advertising Age*, December 7, 1992.

CHAPTER 6

A Day in the Life of an Advertising Agency

Suppose this is your situation. You majored in communications at college, taking related courses in graphic arts, writing, and marketing principles. You spent two summers at a boring job in the advertising department of a small department store in your hometown where most of what you did was run errands to the printer and the local newspaper.

After graduation you toyed with the idea of getting an M.B.A. but decided to put it off, opting instead for a shot at a job in a New York advertising agency. This wasn't easy, but fortunately a close friend of your Principles of Advertising instructor worked at a large New York agency. You weren't the best student in the class, but the instructor liked you enough to write a letter of recommendation to his friend. This was followed up with letters, a résumé, and phone calls, and one day you got a letter from the agency's human resources department inviting you to an interview—at your own expense. All went well at this meeting, and wonder of wonders, you got a job at the agency as an assistant account executive on an airlines account at $16,000.

By sharing an apartment in the warehouse fringe of Greenwich Village with two other recent graduates, you were able to survive.

It wasn't much of a job—mainly typing reports and making phone calls for your boss, an account executive—but it gave you the opportunity to find out how an ad agency functions. You were determined to succeed and even had a timetable of how long it would take to become an account supervisor and outrank your boss.

Here's what a day in your early agency career might look like:

This day is important because it has now been a month since the client, a major airline, approved the media plan. In the coming weeks, the plan must be implemented. The plan calls for a medium-sized TV and radio budget, a major newspaper push, and some outdoor advertising at airport locations. Since deregulation, most airline campaigns emphasize price cutting, and your client is no exception.

In the office of everyone in the airline's account group—account-management, creative, media, and research people—one can see copies of full-page ads for your airline's most recent newspaper campaign, along with those of its competitors. How to be original is the challenge, since most airline advertising stresses either price or service.

After four months on the job you now have the day-to-day responsibility of monitoring the flow of work for the account from each department and reporting back to your immediate boss (the account executive) and her superior (the account supervisor) on its progress. On this day you begin your rounds.

Your first stop is to see the associate creative director on this airline account, who informs you that everything is proceeding apace. He suggests that you drop in on the copywriter, who is just then meeting with an art director to plan the series of full-page newspaper ads. The thrust: Other airlines *talk* about low fares but really have many restrictions; your airline *delivers* low fares. You look at sample layouts and are impressed.

Then you hurry down the hall to the radio department where another copywriter is working on a group of thirty- and sixty-second spots that will be used in all the major cities along this airline's routes.

The same approach taken in print is repeated—*legitimate* low fares. The radio people are also working with a free-lance music outfit on doing a new jingle for the radio commercials.

The in-house TV producer and her staff are working on a series of thirty-second spots. This constitutes a key part of the budget. It means coordinating with an art director who is doing the storyboards, a copywriter doing the scripts, a director, and an outside production house to actually shoot the commercials as well as the agent for the star who will appear on camera. Of course, you will bring the client up-to-date on every phase of this key operation.

Down another floor you go to the media department. The media buyer is meeting with a newspaper rep who is proposing a twenty-city buy with a twice-a-week frequency for a month. Your buyer knows it will be too costly and must cut the budget back.

At that moment the associate media director is lunching at the Four Seasons with a broadcast rep from John Blair. Companies such as Blair represent a large number of TV and radio stations that do not have their own sales force in New York. This rep is putting together a package for the agency's airline account that will include ten- and thirty-second TV commercials as well as thirty-second radio spots to be broadcast during commuting hour (drive time). You have a ham-and-cheese sandwich at your desk.

In the afternoon you pay a visit to the research department. The research people seem to work at a slower pace. They are consulting their data reports to locate the best target audience for budget vacation travel. They use statistics the client has provided plus material they have received from outside market-research specialists.

When you report all your findings to your boss, the account executive, you get an oral pat on the back and are told to continue the good work. Thus endeth the day.

All is well until a week later, when you and your boss visit the client. The airline company is unhappy about the layouts of the print ads and is not sure of the creative thrust of the TV commercials. So it's back to the art and copy team, urging them to summon the muse of advertising creativity. There are only ten days before the campaign's deadline. Oh, well, nobody said advertising was going to be easy.

CHAPTER 7

The Creation of
a TV Commercial

Although ad agencies perform most of their business and creative activities in-house, it is not uncommon to use outside specialists for some services. These might include free-lance illustrators and photographers, research organizations, direct-mail specialists, and television-commercial production companies. TV commercial production is a significant area for medium- and large-size agencies.

Many people who watch commercial television have developed the facility of mentally blocking out those pesky TV commercials. Some people actually zap them with their remote controls the way an electronic zapper demolishes mosquitoes on the back porch. The people who make commercials are aware of this, and some are even redesigning commercials to be more like music videos so that if you zap the sound with your remote control, you'll still see the product name and a more or less comprehensible ad. Subliminally or otherwise, they're getting through. You're in their viselike grip. The only way to avoid them is to not watch commercial television.

Making commercials is a big business. TV production costs rose more than 100 percent in the last eight years. In 1991 the average cost for a thirty-second network commercial was almost $200,000. Some, like soft-drink and automobile commercials, have been known to cost as much as $1 million when celebrities are involved.

The top independent commercial directors, such as Bob Giraldi (Miller Lite) and Joe Pytka (Bartles & Jaymes), get more than $10,000 a day. In fact, the average for all directors is $8,500. Also, the fees for using celebrities in commercials may be enormous.

On a commercial shoot the director is "king." Directors of commercials who are not established in the medium are asked by the agency to submit a reel before they are hired. They are judged by their cinematography, sound, pacing, editing, general creativity, and attention to detail.

Here's how TV commercials are created:

The agency's copywriter and art director design commercials in very much the same way comic strips are drawn and written. First, they create a storyboard—a sequence of sketches of scenes approximating the action in the commercial with the spoken message written below each scene. This helps set up the shots and presents at a glance a visual outline of the commercial's structure. The rendering of a detailed storyboard by a professional sketch artist can cost as much as $100 per frame. A detailed storyboard will have a separate panel for each camera setup and possibly several panels to indicate camera movements. It may also include color coordination and styles for costumes, sets, and props.

The storyboard must then be approved by the client before actual production can start. Once it is approved, the copywriter and art director work closely with the agency's TV producer, who coordinates the production elements before filming or videotaping the spot.

The TV producer is a skilled specialist in many fields. He or she prepares a budget and tries to stick to it; chooses the outside director and cameraman best suited to the job; supervises the casting procedure; consults with the set designer; and works right at the director's side when the commercial is shot. Through it all, the producer adheres to a high standard of production values. After the shooting, he or she must follow through with the film editing, sound recording, and music sessions.

The TV producer is involved with the technical, legal, and financial details in making commercials. He or she must also deal with contracts, unions, film studios, actors, musicians, and the toughest nut—the client. The job requires taste, skill, solid creative judgment, and talent.

BROADCAST OPERATIONS

The broadcast-operations department in an agency follows through on the whole process of a commercial from the early creative stage until it is delivered to the stations to be aired. In large agencies, broadcast operations have a big staff. The progress is monitored most closely by a broadcast coordinator. The coordinator works with the copywriter, art director, producer, legal department, account executives, and the production house that directs and actually shoots the commercial.

BUSINESS AFFAIRS

When a commercial has been written and a storyboard prepared, the business-affairs people are consulted on negotiations with talent and the production house. They send out bids, review them, and write contracts. The commercial must also be approved to make sure it meets with broadcast standards. The TV networks and independent stations maintain continuity-acceptance staffs to approve the content of programming and commercials.

Business-affairs people are often lawyers. Their work demands knowledge and experience of every phase of TV commercial production.

CASTING

Agencies employ specialists who handle the casting of actors, musicians, voice-over people, and singers—generically referred to as "the talent." Casting calls are conducted just as they would be for a feature film. Some agencies screen people in studio facilities that rival broadcasting stations' studios. Here radio and TV commercials can be heard and viewed in all stages of completion by agency people and clients.

The equipment in these studios includes film projectors and screens, videotape players and monitors, audiotape players, and slide projectors. These machines are handled and repaired by operators who have been hired for their skill or trained on the job, so one could conceivably be involved in the production of TV commercials with only "technical" training and expertise.

CAREER TIP

As we have seen, many agency specialists are involved in the production of TV commercials. That means many agency jobs for qualified people. Education helps, but practical experience at a film studio, tape studio, TV station, or production house is also essential.

The ad agency pays for the first performance in a commercial at the studio where it is recorded or filmed. If the commercial is used over and over again, the actors are paid residuals by the agency's talent reuse payment department. Residuals are additional pay given to a performer for repeated use of a radio or TV commercial in which the performer appears. Residuals may be very lucrative, earning tens of thousands of dollars for the actors—more if the commercial receives heavy usage. That's why the competition among actors for work in commercials is so keen. Celebrities who do commercials may also be compensated on a "buy out," or flat fee, basis.

These fees have been known to run into six figures and, on occasion, into seven figures. There are talent agents who specialize in representing actors for commercials.

THE OUTSIDE
PRODUCTION COMPANY

The agency people are specialists, but the TV production companies are the *auteurs*. Their special talents can make the commercial an award winner and, at the same time, sell lots of soap or beer.

Giraldi/Suarez Productions are superstars in the realm of TV production. We talked with Phil Suarez of this company. Here are some of his comments on the relationship between the production company and the ad agency:

> Basically, the production company executes the concept. The agency sends in the concept, and the production company handles all the producing. It does the casting, location scouting, costume designing, and takes care of the sets and the music. It sends the budget and the price to the agency for discussion. Often the discussions entail some change in sets, costumes, or locations to reduce the cost. Once the cost issue is settled, the creative work begins, and our director interacts closely with the agency's art director and creative people. However, the commercial director has most of the creative input while shooting the commercial. He is the one who takes the concept and develops it into the thirty- or sixty-second film, so he not only takes care of directing the actors, the lighting, and so on, but also creates the atmosphere of the whole film.
>
> In our Miller Lite campaign, our problem in terms of actors was that the athletes used were not professional actors. They were, on the whole, very cooperative and delighted to be in the commercial, but they caused a lot more work for the director; consequently, the commercials took much longer to shoot. For instance, in the one with Steve Mizerak, the pool player, there is a trick shot that took 180 takes to come out right. That was exhausting. However, such things happen only when you want the extraordinary to take place. Another instance of this was the commercial with

John Madden (former NFL coach and current sports commentator), who had to crash through a wall. The crash had to be just right, and each time it didn't work, the wall had to be built all over again. Special effects are always time consuming and expensive.

From the standpoint of where the action is, New York is a creative hotbed; all the major creative people are there. Commercials are produced mostly in New York, Chicago, and in Los Angeles, at times, because of the weather. Sometimes we shoot in Florida. The rest of the country really doesn't do much, although some cities like San Francisco have talented people doing this job. But New York is the place to be.

This is a huge industry, making and billing hundreds of millions of dollars for TV commercials. There are hundreds of production companies in New York alone, and basically, if you own a camera and print up a card with your name on it and *Production Company* underneath, you're in business. Among all these companies there are two or three dozen who are very, very good.

Regarding directors of commercials, the reason they have not really made the transition into feature films is that the film work— Hollywood—is not open to them. The film community doesn't really want to let people in from this side of the business. It is much easier to go in the other direction; that is, for a feature-film director to start making commercials. If Sidney Lumet decided to do so, people in the commercial community would be very interested. Exceptions to the rule are directors of commercials in England, many of whom have made the transition from commercials to features—Ridley Scott *(Alien; Blade Runner)* and his brother Tony Scott *(Top Gun)*, to name just two.

Source: Interview in *Making It in the Media Professions* by Leonard Mogel (Chester, Conn.: The Globe Pequot Press, 1988), p. 255.

TRAFFIC

When a spot is produced and given its final okay by the agency and the client sponsor, copies are turned over to one of the many broadcast traffic operators for shipment to the networks or stations in time to make air dates.

The average filmed thirty- or sixty-second TV commercial can take a total of seventy to eighty days of production, with fourteen days allotted for concept, script, and storyboard and eleven days for preproduction (casting, building sets, etc.). Videotape commercials take from fifty to fifty-five days, less time than filmed commercials, since there is less time for processing.

The physical stages a TV commercial goes through are similar to those of a feature film. After the cast is selected and the script finalized and approved by the client, a location is chosen. This may be an island in the Caribbean or a sound studio in Manhattan. The production company engages the technical crew.

The directors and producers view the "rushes," which are the unedited results of each day's shooting. Often the client gets in on the act. The next stage is the *work print,* the relatively inexpensive print of all the original camera footage that has been rough-edited and cut to length. Corrections and possible reshooting are decided upon at this stage.

After that is the *answer print,* an edited version of the commercial that may still be edited further. Finally, there are the *release prints.* These are the reels that will be sent to the individual stations for broadcast.

MISCELLANEOUS FACTS
ABOUT TV COMMERCIAL PRODUCTION

As we have seen, broadcast production is a complex area involving many individuals at the agency who are experts in this specialty. Their responsibilities include the business and creative aspects of TV commercials—an effort that is both glamorous and challenging.

• The average cost for the use of talent on a commercial is $8,100; much more when Michael Jackson or Michael Jordan is involved.

• The average creative fee for an original "jingle" is $23,000.

• The average set construction cost is $21,000 per original commercial.

• Forty-four percent of all studio commercials are shot in one day.

• The most expensive commercials to produce are those with animation and special effects. They increase the average cost by more than $100,000.

Source: AAAA. Television Production Cost Survey System. Report of 1991 findings.

CHAPTER 8

A Profile of the World's Largest Agency and a Small Agency

Agencies come in all sizes. In this chapter we look at the world's largest agency and also a small one, with only twenty-one employees.

In 1987 the largest advertising agency was Saatchi & Saatchi. As a result of aggressive acquisitions and consolidations, Saatchi had billings at about $10 billion worldwide.

Very early on Saatchi & Saatchi was determined to ride the global advertising bandwagon. With the rapid rise of multinational companies, it became apparent that the marketing economy could be affected if the same advertising campaign could be used in many different countries, with only cultural and regional changes. As Saatchi & Saatchi reckoned, get the multinational advertising account first, then set up branch agencies all over the world or purchase agencies in those countries.

In just a four-year period, their U.S. barrage began in earnest when they acquired such powerful agencies as McCaffrey and McCall; Dancer Fitzgerald Sample; Backer Spielvogel; and the then tenth-ranking U.S. agency, Ted Bates, for the extraordinary sum of $450 million.

In 1987, Saatchi & Saatchi could boast of these achievements:

- Its U.K. agency worked with six of Britain's top-ten advertisers.
- The U.S. agency handled more number-one brands than any other agency in America.
- The international network did business with more than 50 of the world's top 100 advertisers.

The combined Saatchi & Saatchi operation represented these prestigious clients in three or more countries:

American Motors	Gillette
Avis	IBM
Bacardi	Johnson & Johnson
British Airways	Mattel
Campbell Soup	Nabisco
Chesebrough-Pond's	Nestlé
Citicorp	Nissan
DuPont	Philips
Eastman Kodak	Procter & Gamble

Five years later, they still had more than half these accounts, but there was a new leader.

WPP GROUP: SINCE 1987
THE NEW KING OF THE AD WORLD

The vagaries of the advertising business, the problems of too rapid expansion, client conflicts, and so on, have afflicted Saatchi & Saatchi. By 1992 they were no longer number one worldwide, and their profits and stock value had plummeted. The new top agency holding company, again as a result of acquisitions in a short time, was the WPP Group, controlled by Martin Sorrell, a modest Englishman in his mid-forties. WPP's billings that year exceeded $18 *billion*. How he did it is a case study for a graduate business school.

Martin Sorrell went to Cambridge to study business. There he wrote a financial column for a college paper and also ran an investment club. In 1964, at the age of nineteen, he came to the United

States to cover the Democratic Convention. While in the States he visited Harvard and applied to the business school. Accepted, he thrived in its trade-school atmosphere.

After graduation he went to work for a consulting firm, starting at the bottom. His next job was for a sports management firm headed by Mark McCormack. McCormack sent him back to London to set up a branch of his company there.

A couple of jobs later, our hero found himself at the newly formed Saatchi & Saatchi organization, which had just taken over the Compton Advertising Group. Since neither of the Saatchis were numbers people, they hired Sorrell as financial director. It was a fortuitous move for Saatchi as well as for Sorrell. Saatchi gained a brilliant financial mind; Sorrell learned the ad business. He put their house in shape at the crucial period in which they were stalking wild boar and acquiring companies at a frenzied pace. He accomplished this by installing financial systems in the companies Saatchi & Saatchi had taken over, raising profit expectations, and applying general financial discipline.

In 1985, while still a Saatchi employee, he bought control of a small public company that made wire and plastic products for supermarkets—WPP, get it?—and sold a piece to the Saatchi brothers. In March 1986, Martin Sorrell left Saatchi and went out on his own, with WPP Products as his public vehicle.

After missing out on bids to take over fifteen companies, Sorrell set his sights on big game, taking on the giant J. Walter Thompson (JWT), 125 years old, with billings of $4 billion. At that time, JWT had run into financial problems. Having raised money for the Saatchis, Sorrell had established marketable contacts in the investment community and proceeded to put them to use in his hostile-takeover bid for JWT. The price—$560 million. The *London Times* in 1987 called it "arguably the most spectacular business deal in memory by a British businessman in America."

In 1989, Sorrell followed this coup with another takeover, this one for the prestigious ad firm of Ogilvy & Mather. Snubbed at first by the acerbic David Ogilvy, he bagged this blue chip with an $862 million bid.

In four years Martin Sorrell built WPP from scratch to the world's largest advertising and public relations organization. WPP's health depends on its various marketing companies and their ability to achieve success for their clients and their brands.

WPP's frenzied buying of companies propelled it to the top of the advertising world but left it saddled with a mountain of debt. In 1991 the economic downturn in Britain and the United States and its concomitant reduction in ad spending resulted in lower profits for the company. Drastic cost-cutting measures were necessary to stave off a cash crisis.

To better understand a goliath such as WPP, let's examine some of its larger elements and their positions as of this writing:

J. Walter Thompson
Founded in 1864, JWT is the fifth-largest advertising agency in the world, with billings of over $4.9 billion. It employs a little over seven thousand people and has 177 offices in forty-two countries. It handles the advertising for thirty-four clients in five or more countries. JWT has separate agency divisions specializing in the fields of health care, recruitment, and direct (the preparation of direct-mail campaigns).

JWT's top ten clients, which represent 35 percent of its income, are the following:

Bristol-Myers	Kraft General Foods
De Beers	Nestlé
Ford	Unilever
Kellogg	U.S. Sprint
Kodak	Warner-Lambert

Companies such as Kraft General Foods are represented by many different agencies for their large variety of brands.

Ogilvy & Mather Worldwide
O&M was founded in 1948 by the advertising luminary David Ogilvy. It is the sixth-largest advertising and marketing group in the world, with billings of almost $4.8 billion. It employs over eight thousand employees in 278 offices in fifty-three countries. It handles the advertising for fifty companies in five or more countries.

As a result of acquisitions, WPP controls other large agencies: Scali McCabe Sloves (nineteenth worldwide); the Minneapolis-based Fallon McElligott; and Cole & Weber, a large West Coast agency.

THE WORLD'S TOP WOMAN AD EXECUTIVE

Charlotte Beers, a math and physics graduate of Baylor University, spent her first ten years in the business world on the client side of advertising, working for a subsidiary of the Mars Company. There she learned how to market the company's Uncle Ben's Rice and other food products. After rising to the rank of group product manager, she joined the J. Walter Thompson Chicago office in 1970 as an account executive.

At JWT her packaged goods experience led to an assignment as senior account director responsible for four of the agency's top clients: Sears, Kraft, Oscar Mayer, and Gillette. Later, the dynamic, plain-spoken Texas native became JWT's first female senior vice president.

But ever onward with Charlotte Beers. In 1979, at the age of forty-three, she moved across town in Chicago to another large agency, Tatham-Laird & Kudner. In just three years at Tatham, Beers became CEO, and in 1991 engineered the agency's successful merger with the Paris-based EURO RSCG, thereby creating the sixth largest agency group worldwide. In her ten-year stint as CEO, she quadrupled the agency's billings while building the revenues of such clients as Procter & Gamble, Nestlé, and Ralston Purina.

The move to the top spot at Ogilvy Worldwide came after a hard-sell courtship by the agency's founder, the legendary David Ogilvy, now in retirement in France. Charlotte Beers's success offers encouragement to all women in advertising. She proves that there are no limits to how far a woman of talent can go in this field.

O&M's top-ten clients, which represent 32 percent of its income, are as follows:

American Express	Ford
AT&T	Kraft General Foods
Campbell Soup	Philip Morris

Philips   Shell
Seagrams   Unilever

Ogilvy & Mather Worldwide also includes O&M Direct (for direct mail).

In addition, WPP Group owns three major public relations firms: Hill & Knowlton, number two in worldwide ranking; Ogilvy, Adams & Rinehart Group, number four worldwide; and Carl Byoir & Associates, a leader in public affairs and public relations for sixty years.

WPP also owns smaller companies in these fields:

corporate and financial-services advertising
corporate travel
custom market research
design
design communications
entertainment-industry advertising
government affairs
health-care marketing
Hispanic marketing and advertising
identity programs
opinion research
promotion marketing
real estate advertising
recruitment advertising
sales promotion
strategic marketing
survey research
travel and leisure advertising
video and audiovisual communications

If our reader at this point is numbed with the size of the WPP Group, other conclusions come to mind. Joining such an organization presents outstanding opportunities. Just as the company engages in cross-referral, integrating the activities of its many arms, so does it nurture talent. A star at one WPP company will be recognized, with the opportunity to become a superstar at another of its companies.

Martin Sorrell, a man who never wrote an ad in his life, has been able to succeed so brilliantly because he is able to motivate management to work for him. He has the business acumen many creative entrepreneurs lack, yet he respects creative people and rewards them well.

A few words here about bigness while we are examining the largest agencies in the world. What is it like working for one of these giants? What are the pros and cons of a large versus a small agency?

On the basis of size alone, a great deal of impersonality exists at large agencies. Someone working on the cavernous third floor of JWT may go out for lunch with the person three cubicles away but have a less than nodding acquaintance with his fellow employees fifty feet from his desk.

THE ADVANTAGES OF A LARGE AGENCY

Here are seven advantages in working for a giant agency:

1. Promotion from within is a common practice.

2. There are more opportunities for women. Of the 107 executives of the rank of vice president and above at J. Walter Thompson New York, almost half are women.

3. Working on a packaged-goods account is a steppingstone to success. A large agency such as J. Walter Thompson handles the advertising for hundreds of packaged-goods products manufactured by some of the most prestigious advertisers in the world.

4. Promotion to a branch office with greater responsibility. From associate creative director in New York to group creative director in Detroit would be a typical situation.

5. As a general rule, large New York agencies pay better than do middle-sized agencies in New York or small-to-middle-sized ones elsewhere.

6. When job switching, it always helps to have gained one's experience at a top-ten agency.

7. With or without a training program, one can usually learn more about one's specialty working for a large agency.

A PROFILE OF A
SMALL ADVERTISING AGENCY

We have had an extensive look at the world's largest agency group. Now let's look at a small one.

E. B. LANE & ASSOCIATES, INC.
733 W. McDowell, Phoenix, AZ 85007
Tel.: 602-258-5263
Telefax: 602-257-8128

Employees: 22   Year founded: 1961

National Agency Associations: AAAA-MAAN

Approx. Annual Billing: $12,000,000

Breakdown of Gross Billings by Media:
Newsp. $2,000,000; Mags. $100,000; POP
    $200,000; Pub. Rels. $500,000; DM
    $200,000; Outdoor $800,000; TV $4,000,000;
    Radio $2,000,000; Production $1,000,000;
    Collateral $500,000; Point of Sale $200,000;
    Consumer Publs. $100,000; Cable TV
    $300,000; Trade Shows $100,000

Edward B. Lane .... Pres.
Gary Vulcano............................ V.P.
Diane Lane..................... Pub. Rels. Dir.
Robin LeMarr .... Media Dir.
Russ Dopke .... Creative Dir.
Diane Fitch .... Office Mgr.
Acct. Execs.: Carolyn Keys, Diane Lane, Beau
    Lane, Ed Coyoli, Jayne Lewis.
Source: *Standard Directory of Advertising Agencies.*

The award-winning agency E. B. Lane & Associates has been in business for more than thirty years, which no doubt attests to its profitability. Its AAAA affiliation is another sign of the agency's stability. MAAN stands for the Mutual Advertising Agency Network, a national networking organization that enables local agencies to have "branch offices" all over the country.

CLIENT LIST

Arizona Dept. of Transportation	Motorola Secure Telecommunications
Cigna Healthplan of Arizona	National Center for Outcome Based
Cowboy Artists of America	Education
Dairy Queen (retail)	The Olive Garden Italian Restaurants
Design Master Homes	Paramount Pictures
EMS, Inc.	PDS (Walsh America)
FM Services Corporation	Popular Stores
First State Service Corporation	Samuel Goldwyn Company
Grossman Properties	Scott Toyota
Marriott's Camelback Inn	Smitty's Super Valu, Inc.
Marriott's Mountain Shadows	Weight Watchers of Arizona

With agencies in smaller markets, management often chooses to remain small rather than face the volatility of having large accounts.

Lane's $12 million in billings fall into fourteen categories. Let's familiarize ourselves with these various media:

1. Newspaper advertising ("Newsp.") placed by the agency gets $2 million in annual billings, while local magazines receive only $100,000.

2. "Mags." refers to advertising placed in trade or business magazines.

3. "POP" refers to "point of purchase," an area we discussed in an earlier chapter. Here Lane's billings reflect their design work on display material in stores and other outlets.

4. "Pub. Rels." (public relations) is a service provided by Lane for its advertising clients and others. These arrangements usually call for a fixed fee per month.

5. "DM" stands for direct mail. Lane performs art and copy service for its clients' mailings.

6. "Outdoor" relates to billboards and other signs used by Lane's clients.

7. "TV" represents Lane's largest billings. The agency writes and directs its own TV commercials and uses production companies for their preparation.

8. "Radio" refers to Lane's client billings in this medium.

9. "Production" relates to billings for art, layout, TV, and radio-commercial production.

10. "Collateral" is the cost of the agency's preparation of miscellaneous materials, such as booklets, brochures, and the like, for clients.

11. "Point of Sale" is similar to point of purchase. It refers to displays in retail stores and the fees paid to retailers for preferred display positions.

12. "Consumer Publs." is the advertising placed in magazines for the general public.

13. "Cable TV" is advertising placed in this medium.

14. "Trade Shows" refers to setting up exhibits for clients at conventions and trade shows.

There are only six executives listed out of the agency's total complement of twenty-two people. Five people are assigned as account executives, one of whom also handles the agency's public relations activity.

E. B. Lane has eighteen listed accounts, the largest of which is Paramount Pictures.

Note that the agency does ad placement and promotion/publicity for two film companies on a regional basis. Their overall client mix is typical for an agency of this size.

THE ADVANTAGES OF A SMALL AGENCY

In a large agency, you are in constant fear of major account losses that may affect your job stability. In a small agency employees often spend their entire careers with a single agency. If you are employed as an account executive at a small agency, you will be integrally involved in the research, media selection and purchase, and creative process for your clients. The learning process is advanced considerably.

Furthermore, small agencies exist everywhere there are advertisers, while large agencies are headquartered in cities such as New York and Chicago.

One may enjoy an excellent life-style working in advertising in a city such as Phoenix or Indianapolis.

The principal disadvantages of working for a small agency are the loss of an opportunity to work on packaged-goods accounts, lower salaries, and the ability to move to other groups and departments within the same agency.

CAREER TIP

If you are willing to work in a big city, such as New York or Chicago, it is probably best to go the big-agency route; the salaries are better and the chances to switch jobs more plentiful. By virtue of the numbers, it's easier to get a job in a big agency. In a smaller city, at a small agency, you will have the opportunity to gain a broader range of experience; then, if that is your desire, the move can be made to the glamorous big time.

CHAPTER 9

Profiles of
Three Specialist
Agencies

There are large and small agencies. There are also many agencies that specialize in particular areas of advertising.

Although most agencies do not specialize in a particular category of accounts, a substantial number do. The Agency Red Book for October 1991 lists 170 agencies that specialize in direct response, 111 in recruitment, 21 in marketing to African-Americans, and countless others in the fields of health care, Hispanic marketing, media-buying, financial services, resorts and travel, and entertainment. We'll discuss three of these specialist agencies.

WESTERN INTERNATIONAL MEDIA CORPORATION (WIMC): THE ENTERTAINMENT KING OF MEDIA-BUYING AGENCIES

Dennis Holt, a gregarious fifty-four-year-old, broke into advertising as a TV sales rep. He founded WIMC in 1970 with a staff of two—himself and an assistant—and three clients. Today he has over seven hundred employees in twenty-five offices and bills over $1 billion a year. His is the country's biggest independent media service company. But to understand his business, we must first understand why advertisers need media-buying agencies when they already use full-service agencies, often with large media departments.

Let's focus on WIMC's most important client, the Disney company. Disney, as we know, is a diverse organization combining the Disney Channel, Disney Home Video, Disneyland, Disney World, and Disney and Touchstone Pictures. The budget for a major Disney movie release may be as much as $15 million spread out over a hundred cities, using TV, radio, newspapers, and occasionally outdoor billboard advertising. Disney's in-house advertising department or one of its agencies will have the responsibility for the creative function, but what about the ad placement?

Along comes WIMC out of the Hollywood Hills, with its six guns ablazing. WIMC is a specialist. Media strategy, research, planning, and buying is their whole business. In the Los Angeles market alone, WIMC buys about 25 percent of all the spot TV available and is by far the largest single buyer in that market. As a result, they can buy the time and space more efficiently and more economically than a full-service agency. That's why Disney uses them. WIMC also buys media for about sixty agencies that represent some fifteen hundred clients.

Another factor is that spot TV and radio prices are negotiable, and negotiating is what WIMC's complement of a hundred full-time buyers and assistants do best. They also benefit because they buy over $400 million a year in spot TV and about $190 million in network, cable, and syndication TV. WIMC has thirty-six former media directors of major agencies on staff.

Disney, spending about $150 million a year, is WIMC's largest client, but they also service about twenty-four other accounts.

Supporting this complex buying and research activity is a computer system that WIMC calls its "Time Machine." It has storage-capacity potential of 40 billion characters, or 14.2 million pages of text.

CAREER TIP

There are major media-buying services in other cities, particularly in New York. Media buying provides a well-paid career for a large number of specialists with a statistical and computer background.

NELSON COMMUNICATIONS, INC.: SPECIALISTS IN HEALTH-CARE MARKETING AND COMMUNICATIONS

Marion Merrell Dow, a major pharmaceutical company, had 1991 sales of $2.85 billion and a net income of $585 million. It spends vast amounts of research money developing new drugs. When a company such as this one is successful with a new drug, its sales for that drug may reach more than $500 million annually. However, this result is not achieved without the expenditure of substantial sums on marketing and advertising.

In promoting a new drug, the pharmaceutical company faces many options. Where should it position the marketing and advertising for the drug? What sampling techniques should it use to bring the drug to the attention of busy medical practitioners? How should the PR campaign be focused on medical professionals and the general public. How should the drug be marketed abroad?

For many of the marketing, public relations, and advertising responsibilities on its new drug, Marion Merrell Dow may call upon one of its agencies, Nelson Communications, Inc., the largest advertising and PR agency in the health-care communications field. In business only since 1987, Nelson today has billings of almost $250 million and operates through an integrated network of eleven subsidiary divisions combining advertising, marketing, and public relations services.

Each of Nelson's eleven subsidiaries performs specialized functions. For example, before a new drug is released to the market, NCI Consulting, one of their subsidiaries, may advise the client regarding strategic planning, market analysis, and advertising positioning. RWR Advertising creates the advertising, which might appear in a dozen professional journals. Another subsidiary, Professional Detailing Network, organizes and manages a sampling campaign to practitioners, while their Pharmacy Sales Network handles sampling and distribution to thirty-five hundred leading independent pharmacies. Nelson's MediScience Associates concerns itself with such heady matters as government regulatory guidance, product-feasibility evaluation, and crisis management in the event of reports of product failure. Finally, NCI Public Relations provides global medical communications and medical educational programs for physicians.

Graphics Corp. of America, another Nelson subsidiary, is a fully computerized production operation providing clients with graphic design and video programs using today's most sophisticated technology. The company also conducts an internship program with Cornell University to provide college students with training in the graphic arts.

Nelson's complement of about five hundred people serves a list of forty clients, including such giants as Merck and Marion Merrell Dow, as well as a number of biotechnology companies.

What kind of background does one need to make it in the challenging field of health-care advertising and public relations? Nelson's staff includes people from journalism, business, regulatory agencies, science, research, and public policy. Many have come from product management at client companies. (We discuss the discipline of product management in some detail later in this book.)

Nelson's top executives come from diverse backgrounds. One of its principals is a former commissioner of the Food and Drug Administration, another a former ad-agency president. Two come from the corporate ranks; and Wayne Nelson, the CEO, was a top executive at Johnson & Johnson.

There are about seventy-five ad agencies specializing in health-care marketing. It is a high-paying, dynamic field, one that is generally not as affected by adverse economic conditions as are consumer-oriented advertising agencies.

OGILVY & MATHER (O&M) DIRECT: THE LARGEST DIRECT-MARKETING AGENCY

Perhaps the best way to understand direct marketing is to give examples of what it does. Here are some of its uses:

- *Direct mail* involves the creation and distribution of sales messages through the mail by businesses, charities, political organizations, and other direct marketers.
- *Telemarketing* uses telephone sales techniques to sell goods and services.
- *Couponing* relates to the preparation of group or "piggyback" mailings to deliver discount coupons to the consumer.
- *TV and radio direct response* entails the production of commercials used to generate direct sales or leads that may be translated into sales.
- *Print direct response* is similar to broadcast, but instead uses coupon ads and card inserts in magazines and newspapers to create sales.
- *Direct marketing* in the yellow pages uses advanced marketing practices to develop results for advertisers.
- *Target marketing* uses data-based strategies to personalize the mailer or advertiser's message to the consumer.

Of these examples of the services of a direct-marketing agency, direct mail receives the greatest budgetary share. It is a giant field, with more advertising spending than television. To better understand the agency's involvement in direct mail, let's consider a typical mailing piece for the American Express Gold Card, a client of our profiled agency, O&M Direct. All figures used in this example are estimated and do not relate to an actual American Express mailing.

Many people will take part in this mailing in which the client's objective is 100,000 new members. First, account management people from the agency meet with the client to define the approach and guidelines of the mailing. The client will then fix the budget—$3 million. This figure translates to the mailing of 5 million pieces at a cost of $600 per thousand and a desired response rate of 2 percent.

Once the budgetary phase is agreed upon, the creative staff begins the process of writing and designing the mailing piece. The client approves each stage in this process. At the same time, the research people at the agency are prospecting for rentable mailing lists that will be used in test mailings. Meanwhile, the agency's production staff is getting estimates on the cost of producing and mailing the piece.

Testing is the operative word in direct mail. With sophisticated research techniques, agencies like O&M Direct are able to measure the relative effectiveness of a mailing package—before it mails. This ensures that the proposed yield will be reached at the budgeted figure.

What makes direct marketing such a challenging specialty is that it is so result oriented. Although all advertising must sell, it is often not measurable. With direct marketing there is no place to hide. Direct-marketing agencies put themselves on the line every day with every project. A client accepts few excuses from its agency for a failed mailing.

Of the 170 ad agencies engaged in this demanding specialty, O&M Direct leads the pack. Their network comprises forty-four offices in thirty-four countries, including eight in the United States. The agency employs about sixteen hundred people worldwide and has total billings of over $820 million. Its client roster includes American Express; AT&T; Kraft; Sears, Roebuck and Company; and the Quality Paperback Book Club.

As we have seen in our example, the staff of a direct-marketing agency like O&M Direct is involved in many of the same functions as a traditional agency: creative, account management, media planning, production, and research. In addition, direct-marketing agencies are heavily involved in computer-software design and marketing systems.

O&M Direct conducts an extensive training program. Another favorable aspect of working for this agency is job stability. The agency seeks out the best people, gives them the tools to do their best, and pays them well. In this way they are able to retain the top talent.

There is far less job switching in direct marketing than at conventional agencies. It is therefore worthwhile to investigate the field of direct marketing. For a list of these agencies, consult the *Standard Directory of Advertising Agencies.*

CHAPTER 10

Who's Hot, Who's Big

WHO'S HOT?

Each year the advertising trade publication *ADWEEK* makes its choices of the thirty hottest ad agencies. The rankings are based on a formula that takes into account overall billings, growth, number of clients lost and new ones gained, growth from current clients, creativity, and management savvy.

When an agency is hot, it draws new clients and top personnel as well. Everyone wants to go with the winner. But we must emphasize that advertising is a very volatile business. An agency that's red hot one year can turn tepid or cool the next. All it takes is the loss of one major account. As *ADWEEK* points out, a number of agencies on this hottest list are newcomers; many of the previous year's winners have dropped off the list. Here is *ADWEEK's* 1992 list (1991 figures):

THE THIRTY HOTTEST AGENCIES

AGENCY	HEADQUARTERS	1991 BILLINGS	RANK AMONG TOP 100 AGENCIES
1. Messner Vetere Berger Carey Schmetterer	New York	$207,835,000	40
2. Goodby, Berlin & Silverstein	San Francisco	117,300,000	75
3. Lewis & Gace	Fort Lee, N.J.	83,064,000	99
4. Wieden & Kennedy	Portland, Oreg.	168,000,000	52
5. Avrett, Free & Ginsberg	New York	245,000,000	35
6. Team One Advertising	El Segundo, Calif.	183,500,000	44
7. Gross Townsend Frank Hoffman	New York	104,586,000	79
8. The Richards Group	Dallas	180,000,000	46
9. Bernstein-Rein Advertising	Kansas City	135,395,000	68
10. Klemtner	New York	165,000,000	54
11. Ferguson Communications Group	Parsippany, N.J.	173,090,000	49
12. Angotti, Thomas, Hedge	New York	90,000,000	89
13. Tatham/RSCG	Chicago	324,679,000	27
14. Rotando Lerch & Iafeliece	Stamford, Conn.	85,500,000	96
15. Kresser/Craig	Los Angeles	92,166,000	87
16. William Douglas McAdams	New York	155,500,000	58
17. Hill, Holliday, Connors, Cosmopulos	Boston	357,293,000	23

18. Arnold Fortuna Lane	Boston	85,590,000	95
19. Admarketing	Los Angeles	317,200,000	28
20. Medicus Intercon	New York	227,748,000	38
21. Wells, Rich, Greene, BDDP	New York	923,700,000	15
22. Margeotes Ferttita & Weiss	New York	103,000,000	82
23. Tucker Wayne/ Luckie & Co.	Atlanta	167,000,000	53
24. Fallon McElligott	Minneapolis	110,000,000	77
25. Mullen	Wenham, Mass.	96,210,000	85
26. Grey Advertising	New York	1,553,000,000	8
27. Geer, DuBois	New York	150,000,000	61
28. Venet Advertising	New York	124,900,000	73
29. Rubin Postaer & Assoc.	Los Angeles	180,700,000	45
30. Rumrill-Hoyt	Rochester, N.Y.	99,350,000	84

Average billings—ten hottest $142,468,000
Average billings—top thirty 233,544,000

Source: "The Thirty Hottest Agencies of 1991," *ADWEEK*, March 23, 1992, p. 13.

What does this listing tell us?

For one thing, New York clearly dominates. Twelve of the thirty hottest have headquarters there. Only one of the thirty hottest is a giant agency, with billings in excess of $1 billion a year.

The number-one agency on this list is Messner Vetere Berger Carey Schmetterer. In 1991 it didn't make the thirty-hottest list.

Number two on this list is Goodby, Berlin & Silverstein, a San Francisco agency that only ranks seventy-fifth on the list of 100 top-billing agencies.

The number-four agency, Wieden & Kennedy, based in Portland, Oregon, with an office in Philadelphia, has gained its hot spot on the basis of its trend-setting advertising for Nike. In June 1991 the agency picked up the $70 million Subaru of America business. Their gain for the year—66 percent.

THE BIGGIES

In 1992 the thirty biggest agencies, based on domestic billings, were as follows:

THE THIRTY BIGGEST AGENCIES

AGENCY	HEADQUARTERS	TOTAL DOMESTIC BILLINGS (1991)
1. Foote, Cone & Belding	Chicago	$2,165,753,000
2. Leo Burnett Co.	Chicago	2,040,268,000
3. D'Arcy Masius Benton & Bowles	New York	1,961,000,000*
4. Saatchi & Saatchi Advertising	New York	1,908,900,000
5. Young & Rubicam	New York	1,852,600,000*
6. J. Walter Thompson	New York	1,753,000,000*
7. DDB Needham	New York	1,688,689,000
8. Grey Advertising	New York	1,553,000,000*
9. Ogilvy & Mather	New York	1,533,200,000
10. BBDO	New York	1,527,220,000*
11. McCann Erickson	New York	1,400,000,000
12. Bozell	New York	1,170,000,000*
13. Backer Spielvogel Bates	New York	1,078,408,000
14. Lintas: USA	New York	1,061,000,000*
15. Wells, Rich, Greene BDDP	New York	923,700,000
16. Campbell-Mithun-Esty	Minneapolis	906,780,000
17. Ayer	New York	754,413,000
18. Ketchum Advertising	Pittsburgh	652,400,000
19. Della Femina McNamee	New York	624,000,000
20. Chiat/Day/Mojo	Venice, Calif.	568,000,000
21. Earle Palmer Brown	Bethesda, Md.	417,350,000
22. Tracy-Locke	Dallas	395,400,000

23. Hill, Holliday, Connors, Cosmopulos	Boston	357,293,000
24. Jordan, McGrath, Case & Taylor	New York	350,000,000
25. Lowe & Partners	New York	325,000,000
26. Hal Riney & Partners	San Francisco	325,000,000
27. Tatham/RSCG	Chicago	324,679,000
28. Admarketing	Los Angeles	317,200,000
29. TBWA	New York	303,728,000*
30. Ally & Gargano	New York	300,000,000

*Estimated billings.
Source: "The Thirty Biggest Agencies of 1991," *ADWEEK*, March 23, 1992, p. 20.

The first fourteen agencies on this list had billings of at least $1 billion a year; the last agency on the list had billings of about $300 million. In an industry with such frequent account changes, total billings are not the whole story. Small agencies turn out advertising as good as the biggies. Accounts are lost for many reasons: The client is acquired, and its advertising is handled by the parent company's agency; sales fall off, and the agency is fired; or the client hires a new management team that wants a new agency.

This points up the precariousness of the agency business. You get a job as an account executive at a hot agency, develop a strong relationship with the product manager on your account, and both the client and your agency group head think you're doing a good job. One day the president of the client company plays golf with the top executive of another agency who tells him what great creative work they're turning out. You guessed it. The account switches agencies, and you're either out of a job or out of that account.

This does happen in advertising, but consider: You may be the hot account executive at the agency that *picks up* the new business. You then become account supervisor on the account and get to play golf with the client.

CHAPTER 11

The Agency Scene
Outside New York

Many of the top advertising agencies are located outside of New York City. Similarly, many of the leading national advertisers are headquartered in cities beyond the Big Apple. One can fashion a fine career in advertising, on the agency or the client side, in many parts of the country.

As an indication of where advertising is centered, here is a chart from the trade publication *Advertising Age* showing the top-ten cities in terms of the total dollar amount of advertising placed by agencies.

TOP-TEN CITIES BY AD BILLINGS

CITY	1991 BILLINGS (in $ thousands)
1. New York	$23,400,000
2. Chicago	7,000,000
3. Los Angeles	4,081,000
4. Detroit	3,648,000
5. San Francisco	1,658,000
6. Dallas–Ft. Worth	1,178,000

7. Minneapolis	1,100,000
8. Philadelphia	936,400
9. Atlanta	895,800
10. Boston	810,200

Source: Reprinted with permission from *Advertising Age,* April 13, 1992, © Crain Communications, Inc. 1992.

Note the substantial penetration of agencies outside New York, even though many of them are branches of New York agencies.

To give readers some perspective on what exists in advertising *out there,* we are profiling six cities—or, more precisely, their market areas, which include their peripheries. The cities are listed in the order of the number of advertising agencies that operate there. We will discuss the cities in terms of their media resources—newspapers and TV and radio stations—the number of their ad agencies, and the important client advertisers.

A word here about branch agencies. Most of the twenty largest agencies headquartered in New York and Chicago have branch agencies in other cities. These agencies exist for two reasons: to service large clients of the parent agency and to serve local clients in local media. Also, if a New York agency has an automobile client in Detroit, it will certainly have a branch office there to expedite the client's day-to-day needs.

CHICAGO

It's the city of Al Capone, Carl Sandburg, Nelson Algren, John Belushi, and Second City. Its hog-butchering image is a bad rap. Why, the Chicago Cubs even play night games. The city is renowned for its theaters and Art Institute as well as its jazz clubs.

In advertising and media this is the big time. There are thirty-eight radio stations and eight TV stations. Also, twenty daily newspapers cover the area, led by the powerful *Chicago Tribune* (daily circulation: 720,000)* and its not-so-powerful longtime competitor, the *Chicago Sun-Times.*

*All circulation figures listed in this chapter are courtesy of *Inside Media.*

There are about 250 ad agencies in Chicago, including branch offices of almost every large New York–based agency. Foote, Cone & Belding, the number-one agency in domestic billings ($2.1 billion), is based in Chicago, as are Leo Burnett ($2 billion) and Tatham/RSCG ($324 million).

CAREER TIP

The cost of living in Chicago is lower than in New York, especially in the area of affordable housing, yet ad and media salaries are not substantially lower. There are any number of pleasant suburbs if one chooses not to live in town. Chicago may be a good place to make it in advertising.

LOS ANGELES

Although Los Angeles is not quite the boom town it was in the 1970s and 1980s, the lure of the sunshine, the surf, and the glitz keeps the population growing at rapid levels. The Los Angeles five-county Consolidated Metropolitan Statistical Area (CMSA) ranks the area in second place, just after New York, with a population of over 14 million.

What is also inviting about the area is its diversification in recent years. No longer does Los Angeles exist on its cottage industries alone—aerospace, entertainment, and tourism. In terms of employment, business and financial services now rank as the number-one industry.

Anyone planning to pursue an advertising career in the Los Angeles area must give the move careful consideration. The smog and freeway congestion are clearly disadvantages. With the industry spread out all over Los Angeles and Orange counties and no effective rapid transit, round trips from home to the workplace of more than two hours are commonplace. Also, the sharp drops in defense spending in the early 1990s have caused a slump in the economy of the entire Los Angeles area.

Another consideration is salaries versus the cost of living. If you work at an L.A. ad agency or a movie studio, you'll make about the same salary as you would in New York. However, the cost of living is 24.1 percent higher than the national average and about the same as in New York.

Los Angeles is a major media market. In the greater L.A./Orange County region, there are forty-four radio stations and ten commercial TV stations; yet there is only one major daily newspaper, the *Los Angeles Times* (circulation: 1,225,000 daily).

In terms of advertising agencies, it is third in the nation, with about two hundred. Here is a list of the agencies in the top 100 and their 1991 billings:

	NATIONAL RANK	BILLINGS
Chiat/Day/Mojo	20	$568,000,000
Admarketing	28	317,000,000
Team One	44	183,500,000
Rubin Postaer & Associates	45	180,000,000
Dailey & Associates	56	156,000,000
Davis, Ball & Colombatto	63	149,000,000
Eisaman, Johns & Laws	70	131,000,000
Kresser Craig	87	92,000,000

Source: *ADWEEK*, March 23, 1992. Reprinted with permission.

The Los Angeles area is also the headquarters of many large companies that are national advertisers. Your job quest in advertising should certainly include these as possibilities:

Carnation Company
Nissan Motor Company
Toshiba
Toyota Motor Corp.
Walt Disney Company
All the major film studios

SAN FRANCISCO

The sun never comes out before 11:00 A.M., and you may need to wear a sweater in midsummer, but San Francisco certainly has its charms. Some have even called it everyone's favorite city, after their own.

Although the Bay Area is only the fourth-largest population center, with about 6 million people, media abounds. There are forty-nine radio stations and eleven TV stations in the San Francisco–Oakland–San Jose area. Cable TV has a very substantial market coverage. The largest newspaper in the area is the *San Francisco Chronicle,* with a daily circulation of about 570,000.

One should realize the extent of the San Francisco market area. It includes the bay city and also Oakland (2 million population) and San Jose (1,400,000).

San Francisco has been spared some of the economic downturn that has affected Los Angeles, but its cost of living keeps rising rapidly. It has the second-most-expensive housing market in the country, trailing only Honolulu. As a result, the Bay Area has a very high percentage of renters—36.9 percent. Only L.A., with 41.4 percent, and San Diego, with 38.6 percent, exceed San Francisco's rate.

The ad-agency scene is very positive in San Francisco. There are 115 agencies in this market, but only two, Hal Riney & Partners (1991 billings: $325 million) and Goodby, Berlin & Silverstein ($117 million), are in the top 100 in agency billings. In terms of industry, the range is diverse; but high-tech companies, such as those in Silicon Valley, dominate. Other companies that are major advertisers include:

Chevron Corp.
Del Monte Corp.
Gallo Winery
Hunt-Wesson Foods
Levi Strauss & Co.
Sunsweet Growers

INDIANAPOLIS

There is life in Indianapolis beyond the Indianapolis 500. It is a city of 1.25 million that has staged a dramatic comeback in recent years, with a revitalized downtown, low unemployment, and a cost of living a few percentage points below the national average.

Indianapolis has seven TV stations covering its metropolitan area, twenty radio stations, and eighteen newspapers, one of which, the *Indianapolis Star* (a daily), has a circulation of 230,000 weekdays and about 400,000 on Sundays.

There are thirty-two ad agencies in Indianapolis, many of which are branches of New York and Chicago agencies. These agencies service the local needs of national accounts as well as local clients that advertise in local media. Some national companies headquartered in Indianapolis are Eli Lilly, Magnavox, and ITT Educational Services.

DETROIT

Detroit's broader metropolitan area has grown enormously in recent years. No longer is the area's economy totally dependent on the auto makers. Instead, other industries have proliferated to a point where the auto industry employs only 8 percent of the work force.

In the media Detroit's metro area has thirty radio stations, seven TV stations, and a daily newspaper with 1 million circulation. Detroit has thirty ad agencies, including Ross Roy (number 39 in national ranking in terms of total billings). In terms of total advertising billings, Detroit is the fourth-largest city in the nation.

If you live and work in the Detroit area, there is one other significant statistic. The median sales price of an existing single-family house is only $73,700, well below the nation's average of $92,200.

Some major advertisers in Detroit:

Chrysler Corp.
Dow Chemical Company
Ford Motor Company

General Motors Corp.
Kellogg Company
K mart

SEATTLE-TACOMA

It may rain in Seattle, but that hasn't deterred its population growth and the cultural explosion of recent years. Today Seattle-Tacoma, as its market area is designated by the CMSA, is a progressive metropolis with a population in excess of 3.3 million and a national ranking of fifteenth position. If you're considering building your advertising career in Seattle, you'll be pleased to know that there are nine TV stations, including three network affiliates and a Fox affiliate as well. The radio markets number fifty stations, one of which, KING-FM, an all-classical station, is consistently the highest-rated classical station in the country.

The Seattle-Tacoma area has six daily newspapers, including the *Seattle Times* and the *Seattle Post-Intelligencer*, which publish under a joint operating agreement and have a daily circulation in excess of 200,000. The success of an alternative urban newspaper, the *Seattle Weekly* (circulation: 33,000), confirms the city's appeal to a well-educated, upscale audience.

There are a number of general and special-interest magazines published in Seattle. One, called *KCTS Nine,* for public TV subscribers, has a circulation of 160,000. (Sixty thousand copies go to neighboring British Columbia.)

If you want to make it in the advertising-agency world, Seattle offers no fewer than twenty-three agencies. Cole & Weber, its largest agency, is owned by the giant WPP Group and has annual billings of about $83 million. There are eight agencies in the $20–$50 million range.

Before you pack your credentials and hustle to Seattle on the next plane, a word of caution. Seattle has attracted many Los Angeles and San Francisco expatriates fleeing the urban sprawl and high cost of living in those cities. The competition for ad and media jobs has become very keen. Consult the Seattle agency listings in the *Standard*

Directory of Advertising Agencies. There you will find the names of all the top agency personnel. Perhaps one of these people is an alumnus of your college; that's somewhat of an entrée. The listings will also show the names of all the agencies' accounts. You can then begin sending your résumé to the agencies and accounts that interest you. It's a good approach before you make the move.

A major advertiser in the Seattle-Tacoma area is the Boeing Company.

MAKING IT IN OREGON

After ten years in advertising, Debra Weekley is clearly a success story, as is her agency, Wieden & Kennedy. In 1991 it was number four in *ADWEEK*'s list of hottest agencies (see page 77). Wieden & Kennedy's work for Nike on TV and in print has been both admired and copied. Here's what Weekley has to say about making the move from a giant New York agency to a smaller one in Portland, Oregon.

To what extent did your education prepare you for an advertising career?

I was very lucky to have an education that prepared me for a career in advertising. While attending the University of Missouri School of Journalism (which has an emphasis in advertising), I studied with Russ Doerner, who told me that I wouldn't make it as a copywriter, but instead, that I should shift my attention to what I did best: marketing, strategy, and account-management work. At the School of Advertising there were several advertising/marketing competitions that simulated small ad agencies. A few of the professors had experience or good contacts with major ad agencies, so graduates had a name to whom they could pass their résumés.

What has been your career path on the way to your present job as account supervisor at Wieden & Kennedy?

While at college, during summers I worked as a sales representative for General Foods' Kool-Aid/Country Time Lemonade. This seasonal product needed a swat team of college kids during the summer.

From 1982 to 1988 I worked at Dancer Fitzgerald Sample (later to become part of Saatchi & Saatchi Advertising) as an account coordinator on Life Savers products. I was then promoted to assistant account executive on this account. Later, I became an account executive on Parker Brothers toys and then became senior account executive on Northwest Airlines. In 1988 I joined Wieden & Kennedy in Portland, Oregon, as an account supervisor on Nike and KINK Radio. In 1992, I became account supervisor on Pepe jeans and Oregon Tourism as well as KINK Radio.

We see great advertising coming from many cities other than New York and Chicago. Certainly your own agency, Wieden & Kennedy, is a major example of such high creativity. Are salaries generally lower in cities such as Portland, and if so, what are the rewards?

I'm making a bit less than I would in New York or Chicago, but I continually have to tell headhunters that they couldn't pay me enough to move back to New York to work in advertising. The major benefits working in Portland include life-style: living in an incredible and affordable city, surrounded by forests and high mountains. It also means having a savings plan, a car, a house, and lots of great vacations. The work style at a smaller agency focuses on the integrity of the work. Therefore, the great advertising coming from smaller agencies is a result of a more rewarding life-style and a better work environment.

You worked in advertising in New York. What is the principal difference in your work style at Wieden & Kennedy?

My work style here is far more comfortable than it was in New York for two main reasons:

First, after two months in Portland I donated most of my New York power suits and dresses to the Salvation Army. They were uncomfortable and looked geeky at Wieden & Kennedy. My feet are much healthier, since I no longer wear high heels. The world out west is far more casual, comfortable, and real.

Second, I spend less time on the politics that are inherent in a large, multilayered ad agency where one must maneuver his or her way through the hierarchy of creative, media, traffic, and account management to get anything done. People here speak openly and honestly without a concern about what is politically smart.

What kinds of accounts do you service?

Basically, I work with clients who trust me and the agency. I've just moved off supervising the Nike account. During my tenure on this account it grew from $50 million to $120 million. This fast-paced, exciting, growth-oriented account was a lot of fun and a great challenge. The Nike people are some of the bravest I've ever met, always willing to take chances. With packaged-goods clients, an account person may often do the job of a product manager, which entails a great deal of research and analysis. On accounts like Nike, the agency does about thirty ads a year for all of their product lines and seasons.

Pepe jeans has been a fascinating experience. We've spent the last six months conducting research that has helped lead us to a new campaign that will reposition the brand to become a national player among premium jeans (Guess?, Girbaud). Our work has resulted in a campaign that we hope Pepe will use for the next ten years.

Oregon Tourism involves two of my favorite things: Oregon and tourism. It's very rewarding when you can really help the state economy by helping to bring tourists into the state.

KINK radio is a local radio station appealing to baby boomers. It plays a cool, intelligent mix of rock, adult contemporary, and jazz. In a market filled with typically bad radio advertising, KINK's marketing team is one of the smartest I've dealt with in terms of strategy and good sense.

What is the general structure of your present agency in terms of total billings and number of employees?

Wieden & Kennedy presently expects to enjoy billings of $200 million in 1992. We currently have approximately 180 people, 130 in Portland and 50 in Philadelphia.

We have reported that even the largest agencies hire fewer than a dozen new people each year. What would you recommend as the best way to get a job in advertising today?

First of all, consider smaller agencies in smaller cities. Some of the best work is done there. Don't wait for the perfect agency job.

I don't believe any experience is useless in this industry. Some of the best people I've worked with come from such diverse backgrounds as the Peace Corps, acting, teaching, banking, and client-side marketing/advertising jobs.

I'd recommend doing tons of research on the kind of agency job you want most. When you finally get an appointment for an interview, dig up as much information as you can about the company before stepping into a formal interview. As an interviewer, I can always tell if the interviewee has gone out of his or her way to understand the job, the agency, and the type of people with whom they will work. Next, I'd recommend tenacity and finesse. It's important to know how often and how to follow up the interview. Contacts beget contacts. Intelligence, honesty, and enthusiasm do the same thing.

Finally, I'd choose the city I'd like to live in, go there, and then look for a job. I firmly believe that your life outside the job deeply affects your work. I know that most agency jobs are in New York and Chicago, so people may have to start there in order to build their résumés. I think, however, as more talent and businesses recognize the work coming out of smaller markets, it will be much easier to find challenging advertising careers in these markets.

ADVERTISING AGENCIES ABROAD

These days, when one considers employment in an American advertising agency or, more realistically, when one is fortunate enough to be chosen for employment, chances are that the agency will be part of a multinational network. You may be hired in New York as an assistant account executive and six months later be offered a shot as an account executive in the agency's Paris office. Not bad if your salary adjustment affords the expensive Parisian life-style. An ad-agency assignment could also take you to such exotic locales as Melbourne, Capetown, Stockholm, or Istanbul.

As we have discussed, global conglomerations are being formed all the time. These moves make some economic sense. The agency is better able to handle the needs of multinational companies located here and abroad. In fact, two of the giants we have discussed are headquartered in London—Saatchi & Saatchi and Martin Sorrell's WPP Group. At this writing, another English-French group, Aegis Group PLC, has been gobbling up enough agencies to put it in the top-seven ranking among worldwide agency holding companies.

We certainly will see more of this globalization in the 1990s. Of course, there are pros and cons over the efficacy of this activity. In our viewpoint, if it checks the demise of weaker agencies and provides more advertising jobs, it's a positive trend.

ONE WOMAN'S SUCCESSFUL JOURNEY FROM CHICAGO TO TAIPEI

Of the many U.S. agencies that have branch offices around the globe, Leo Burnett, the giant Chicago-based agency, is no exception. In January 1986, Michelle Kristula-Green went halfway around the world to Burnett's Taipei, Taiwan, office to work as an account director on the agency's Procter & Gamble, United Airlines, Hewlett-Packard, and Quaker accounts. How has she fared? The answer: brilliantly.

When Kristula-Green joined Leo Burnett Taiwan, there were only twenty-three people on staff. In two years the agency grew to sixty-eight, but everyone still knew everyone else's name and job responsibility. In this small office environment one account executive handled two or three accounts, and a creative group head was responsible for about fifteen accounts. Much time was spent in meetings, those with clients conducted in Chinese. Fortunately, Kristula-Green speaks Chinese, although some of her colleagues don't speak English.

Here are some comments from Michelle Kristula-Green on what it's like working in Taiwan:

> The Taiwan office does more than develop TV, print, and radio ads. We design packages, sales materials, shopping cartons, and product leaflets. We even get asked to decorate banquet halls for sales meetings. As a result, we can create and maintain a more consistent look for a brand.
>
> Other Burnett offices in Asia are often working on the same brands. As a result, there is a lot of cooperation and sharing of

information between offices—in addition to many opportunities to meet and get to know each other.

In between work (and sometimes in conjunction with it) I've enjoyed taking trips to Hong Kong, Korea, and Thailand. It's as easy as flying to New York from Chicago for the weekend.

Unfortunately, traveling around Taipei isn't as easy. Traffic is chaotic. There are no "rules of the road," and there are as many motorcycles as people.

Despite being a small office and dealing with the difficulties of working in a culture which is very different from the West, the variety of new challenges makes every day unique and exciting.

Kristula-Green made these comments in 1988. The Chinese work style has obviously agreed with her. In 1991 she was still in Taipei, but as a Leo Burnett vice president with many increased responsibilities.

As more and more U.S. agencies go global, opportunities such as these will become more prevalent. A basic requirement—the knowledge of at least one other language and the flexibility to adapt to another culture.

PART III

Advertising Outside the Agency World

CHAPTER 12

An Overview of the Advertising Client

THE CLIENT SIDE

In our discussion of the agency in Part II, we referred to the client or advertiser. (We use the terms interchangeably.) The client assigns the execution of the advertising to the agency. It is the client's role that we explore in this part of the book.

An advertiser is also a marketer. Formally, marketing is the total of activities involved in the transfer of goods from the producer of the product to the consumer, or buyer, *including* advertising and selling. The marketing process comprises:

planning
test marketing
market research
product development
package design
sales promotion
advertising

The advertising agency may become involved in all or some of these activities on behalf of a brand, or product, of the advertiser. However, the agency's principal role is creating the advertising and placing it in the most effective media.

In the process of working with its ad agency, the advertiser decides on an annual advertising budget and the budget for a specific campaign. The advertiser approves every element in the campaign. This will include the media to be used and the amounts to be spent in each medium; the content of each print ad, or TV and radio commercial; and the analysis of the campaign's results.

For example, the pharmaceutical giant Johnson & Johnson's leading product is Tylenol, with annual sales volume of about $600 million. Johnson & Johnson spends about $70 million annually to advertise this brand. The ad agency for Tylenol is Saatchi & Saatchi, who may be involved with test marketing and market development for this product, but whose basic function is creating its advertising.

Johnson & Johnson's marketing staff supervises and coordinates the advertising with Saatchi & Saatchi. They also measure its effectiveness. In this respect, the barometer is sales. If the ad program increases the sales of Tylenol, it works. If not, Johnson & Johnson's marketing staff finds out why it didn't, and then either changes the ad campaign or even possibly fires the agency.

The product management team for Tylenol at Johnson & Johnson performs other marketing tasks besides monitoring the advertising. They are concerned with the product's distribution, packaging, sales promotion, consumer acceptance, pricing, and display. Without proper management of these elements, the advertising cannot be used to full advantage.

Although our example here of Tylenol relates to a "superbrand," a small advertiser has similar responsibilities on a lesser scale. A local advertiser such as an auto dealer may have an annual advertising budget of only $100,000, yet the dealer still looks to its ad agency for sales results. If the agency doesn't achieve these results, the dealer's response may be to change agencies.

What is important to know at this stage is that areas of responsibility at the client are clearly defined. The product and brand managers do not execute the advertising. Instead, they supervise it while performing many other duties in sales and marketing. Clients employ their own people to come up with goals and define their markets. Agencies help them market their products and services. The size of staff and degree of specialization within client companies varies depending on the number of products, budgets, and so on.

JOBS ON THE CLIENT SIDE

If you are interested in pursuing a career on the client side of advertising, you'll be pleased to know:

- salaries average 20 percent more than at an ad agency.
- the agency offers the creative and media recommendations, the client side makes the decisions and has the power.
- jobs on the client side are more stable. When an agency loses an account, a number of account, creative, and media people may be fired. At the client, it is only when a brand is discontinued, a rare occurrence, that marketing personnel are fired.

In the succeeding chapters of this part we will discuss the structure of advertising departments and job descriptions of the people who run these departments.

CHAPTER 13

Structure and Function of a Client Advertising Department

ADVERTISING TASKS AT A LARGE CLIENT COMPANY

T he structure and function of an advertiser's in-house advertising/marketing staff depends on the number of products and size of the company, and varies widely. The chart on page 101 indicates the functions and personnel of a large company's advertising services department. The model used here is for a company with multiple products.

Here is an explanation of the work done by the departments shown in the chart:

Client Management
The top level people at the client who oversee the company's advertising are known collectively as client management. This group decides on the size of budgets and choice of media. A large company that produces many types of products might have an advertising staff as listed on page 102.

ADVERTISING SERVICES

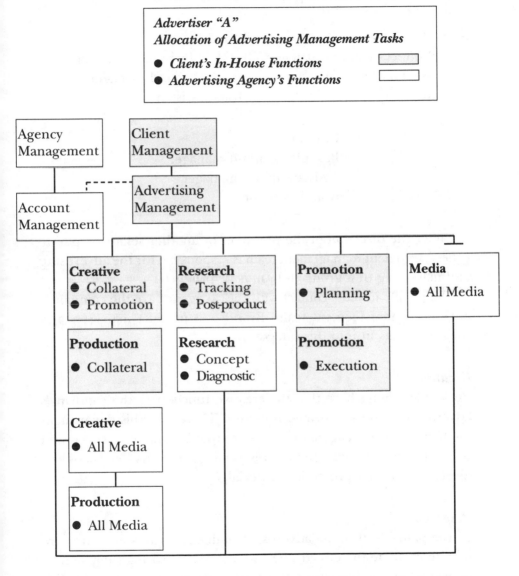

When the decision is made to allocate some of the advertiser's tasks to a full-service agency to perform, the basic structure remains unchanged— only the lines and patterns denoting affiliation have been added.

Source: Reprinted courtesy of ANA and Chuck Jones-Lundin Associates, Inc.

President
Vice president—director of marketing (or advertising)
Associate marketing (or advertising) director

Brand A   Brand B
Product or brand manager   Product or brand manager
Assistant brand manager   Assistant brand manager
Brand assistant   Brand assistant

Brand C
Product or brand manager
Assistant brand manager
Brand assistant

Under the direction of the president or another senior corporate officer, the client management team is responsible for the advertising and marketing of a group of brands or products.

The people in daily contact with the ad agency are the company's advertising management team. Brand and product managers and their assistants fit into this category.

Creative

We are assuming here that the creative function of the company's advertising is not performed in-house. Therefore, this department might review the ad agency's creative output but would be concerned primarily with producing brochures, catalogs, informational booklets, displays, and sales-promotion material.

Research

In companies with large advertising budgets, various measures are used to evaluate the effectiveness of a total advertising campaign or individual ads. Interviews with consumers are a key source for this testing. The in-house staff and the agency direct this research, which is typically carried out by outside specialists.

"Postproduction" research is another method used to test the effectiveness of a TV commercial after it is produced but before it is aired. Test groups of from fifteen hundred to two thousand people see the commercial and comment about it. This is usually a client activity carried out with agency cooperation.

Promotion

The planning of promotional campaigns is a function of the client and is used primarily to promote sales. The client supervises implementation of these programs, which are typically carried out by outside service companies. An example of such a promotion would be a training film produced for a manufacturer's dealers. The agency may or may not be involved in such a promotion, depending on the policies of the client.

Production

The agency carries out the production of broadcast commercials and print advertising. The client's in-house production staff handles production on materials it creates. An example might be the company's participation in an industry trade show. For this event, the production staff is responsible for both the design of the booth itself and the printed materials to be distributed.

HOW THE SIZE OF A COMPANY RELATES TO ITS STRUCTURE

Large companies with multiple divisions and product lines usually maintain larger in-house marketing and advertising staffs than do small companies.

At Levi Strauss, the world's largest apparel manufacturer, the company spends about $160 million a year with a relatively small supervisory staff. Each of their four divisions has an advertising manager and a director of marketing services. These eight people have overall advertising responsibility for the entire company. The product managers at Levi Strauss are concerned with sales and profit but not design and advertising.

Procter & Gamble is our nation's largest advertiser, with a budget exceeding $2 billion a year. The company has eleven divisions and ten subsidiaries. At these divisions and subsidiaries, a senior vice president or vice president of marketing and advertising controls the division's advertising functions. Seventeen advertising agencies have responsibility for the products of these divisions. Some of these agencies have as many as twenty different Procter & Gamble product lines.

Some major companies perform many advertising functions in-house and use agencies only for specialized services; others do not use agencies at all.

CLIENT/AGENCY RELATIONSHIPS

There are various kinds of agency relationships a client may choose to adopt. These relationships vary according to the tasks the client wishes the agency to perform. A common arrangement is for the client to engage a full-service agency; that is, one that provides creative services, media selection and placement, and production. In this relationship, the agency offers recommendations and services, but the client side makes the decisions. In such an arrangement between client and agency, the contact levels are reasonably well defined, usually as follows:

CLIENT	AGENCY
Vice president, marketing/brand management	Management supervisor
Group product/brand manager	Account supervisor
Product/brand manager	Account executive
Supervisor/director of research	Research director
Media manager	Associate media director or media director
Media coordinator	Media planner/buyer

Large client-companies also employ people in the peripheral areas of advertising, such as creative, market research, promotion, media selection, market planning, and production.

CHAPTER 14

Jobs at the Advertising Client Company

The size and extent of client ad departments vary, of course, according to the number of products the company advertises, the size of its budget, and the advertising functions it elects to do in-house, which may include TV and print production and research.

The salaries listed below for each client job classification are subject to many variables and should be taken as general—and rough—ranges. Generally speaking, client salaries average at least 20 percent more than comparable job titles and experience at agencies.

The average salaries listed come from *ADWEEK*'s June 3, 1991, issue and do not include bonuses and perks.

ADVERTISING MANAGEMENT

Vice President, Marketing Services, or Vice President/Director of Marketing

JOB DESCRIPTION. This is a top executive of a company or division of a large corporation who is accountable to the president for all sales and advertising of that unit. Budgeting and control of media expenditures fall within his or her domain.

QUALIFICATIONS. One doesn't reach this level without at least ten years of experience as a product or brand manager. A college major in advertising or marketing is beneficial. An M.B.A. is almost a requirement at a large packaged-goods company.

CAREER PATH. From here, the route is often senior vice president, marketing or sales, and then on to president.

SALARIES. The average for this job is $80,000.

Group Product Manager

JOB DESCRIPTION. In a company with many brands or divisions, this job title is held by an individual supervising two or more product managers. He or she reports to the vice president/director of marketing. According to David Mackay, category director at Kellogg Cereals, "There are very few other positions where you can have as much impact on a given brand or business."

QUALIFICATIONS. At least four years' experience as a product manager is required to attain this job. Here, too, an M.B.A. is excellent preparation.

CAREER PATH. Vice president/director of marketing is the next step up. The path getting there may take eight or ten years.

SALARIES. The average for this job is $60,000.

Product or Brand Manager

JOB DESCRIPTION. Many companies, such as Procter & Gamble, use the product-manager system. The product manager is responsible for the details of marketing the product. He or she works closely with agency account and creative people to steer the advertising messages in the right direction. In addition, product managers also create strategies for the brand and develop marketing plans that include advertising, promotion, and packaging.

QUALIFICATIONS. For large packaged-goods companies, a requirement is at least three or four years' experience in brand management. As with most of these positions, an M.B.A. is the ticket of admission. One needs excellent organizational skills to perform effectively in this area.

CAREER PATH. The next rung up is group product manager. To become a product manager, one usually starts as brand assistant and then assistant brand manager.

SALARIES. The average is $50,000.

Assistant Product or Brand Manager

JOB DESCRIPTION. In addition to assisting the brand manager in all of his or her functions, the assistant may have specific responsibilities regarding media and advertising, meaning more agency contact and less sales and other marketing services.

QUALIFICATIONS. One does not get hired for this job right out of college, even with an M.B.A., unless the job is with a small company. At least two years as an assistant is required.

CAREER PATH. The rise to brand manager may be achieved in just a few years as a brand assistant, or trainee, and another few years as an assistant brand manager.

SALARIES. The average is $40,000.

Assistant Brand Manager and Brand Assistant

JOB DESCRIPTION. As a training position the job runs the gamut of marketing and advertising functions. Detail work rather than planning and decision making is the function of these jobs. The assistant brand manager will also work closely with the agency on ad approvals and budgeting.

QUALIFICATIONS. Although some assistants are hired right out of college, with only a bachelor's degree, an M.B.A. is an advantage.

CAREER PATH. The job of brand assistant is entry-level. Promotion leads to assistant brand manager in a few years. Few make the move to agencies, since they soon realize that life and salaries are richer on the client side.

SALARIES. The average for a brand assistant is $25,000; for an assistant brand manager, it is $30,000.

Other Client Advertising Jobs

SALES PROMOTION. This activity involves contests, posters, giveaways, brochures, and coupons. The job consists of planning, designing, and producing collateral material to create extra interest in the purchase of a product.

DIRECT MARKETING. Direct marketing and direct mail are not confined to specialist advertising agencies. They are also important client activities. The focus of this work is planning, statistics, copywriting, and art direction. Since many of these functions are similarly performed at agencies and by clients, a good deal of job shifting occurs in the field of direct marketing.

Direct marketing has become a hot area of advertising due to technological advances in computers and mailing lists. The field offers a foot in the door to the advertising industry, especially for copywriters and art directors.

SALARIES AT CLIENT JOBS

Men earn substantially more money than women for similar jobs on the client side. Women seem to be as underpaid in this glamorous profession as they are in other management situations. Fortunately, however, the gap is narrowing.

ADWEEK tabulated the salary increases that business and industry marketing executives (not agency) can expect for experience on the job.

JOB CLASSIFICATION	0—5 YEARS	6—10 YEARS	20 + YEARS
Top advertising and sales promotion executive	$40,000	$49,000	$81,000
Advertising manager	31,000	39,000	
Sales-promotion manager	30,000	38,000	
Brand or product manager	46,000	56,000	

Conclusion: Get promoted fast and stay on the job—or go back to school and get an M.B.A.

Source: "1991 Salary Survey Results: Corporations," *ADWEEK,* June 3, 1991.

CHAPTER 15

A Case Study
of a Product Launch

We have discussed the role of the agency and that of the client. Now we will see how they interact when a packaged-goods company prepares a new product for the market.

All new food products are test-marketed. That is, initially they are distributed to a limited number of food stores, and their success or failure there is measured before the company elects to place the products in full distribution.

Suppose a large food company creates an iced cappuccino product. Although the market for such an upscale product is limited, the company has high expectations for it, since there is little competition and it will be high-priced.

The product will be test-marketed by the company's Refrigerated Products Group, headquartered in St. Louis. A series of meetings is held with the group's president; vice president, direct marketing; vice president, strategy and development; vice president, direct sales; and the director of operations and technology. Of course the product itself has already passed through the test kitchen and manufacturing stage. The results show that the product has an excellent taste and can easily be manufactured at the desired price level.

Meanwhile, the food company's package-design people have come up with a label that shows a serene country scene in the background, with a colorful illustration of the iced drink in a glass with a straw. The name of the new product is "Cappuccino Delizioso."

This food company has four ad agencies handling a total line of forty products. A large Chicago agency, which already handles a number of the company's other frozen food products, receives the account assignment. An executive vice president at that agency, its highest-ranking official on this company's account, is invited to a series of meetings, along with the agency's creative director, senior media director, an account supervisor, and the account executive who will be the day-to-day person on this product launch, working closely with the product manager for the brand.

The test-marketing ad budget is pegged at $500,000. This isn't a large amount, but the agency knows that if the test works, the budget will be increased four or five times.

In test-marketing Cappuccino Delizioso, each region or territory receives different advertising media. For example, radio is used in some areas, TV in others, couponing and taste sampling in another territory, or a combination of these marketing procedures in still other markets.

At each step during the test-marketing advertising campaign, the product manager and the agency people closely interact. The product manager at the client company approves the budget, selection of media, and the final content of every print ad and radio and TV commercial. When the test-marketing period is over, the marketability of Cappuccino Delizioso is evaluated and deemed a success.

The new product sells well in upscale suburban areas and specialty food stores in New York, Los Angeles, and San Francisco. TV, used on a limited basis in the test, seems to be more effective than radio or newspaper advertising.

The food company decides to go national with the product for the following spring. There will be some change in the packaging and the pricing. The ad campaign, too, will be changed, with greater emphasis on the slogan "You'll feel like you're in Venice when you drink Cappuccino Delizioso." The ad budget for the new launch period will be $1.2 million.

And so goes our imaginary test-marketing example. Many people on the client and agency side participated, but none as significantly as the client's product manager. He or she is the one individual involved in every phase of the test, and the product will continue to be his or her primary responsibility during the official launch.

CHAPTER 16

The 100 Leading Advertisers

E ach year the publication *Advertising Age* publishes "The 100 Leading National Advertisers" issue. The rankings for this important issue come from various sources, including: LNA/ Arbitron Multi-Media Service, LNA/Media Records, Arbitron, and Publishers Information Bureau. The ad spending referred to in this issue is both measured and unmeasured. Measured media advertising refers to ad expenditures in national consumer media that are monitored by the sources listed above. Unmeasured spending includes direct mail, promotion, couponing, catalogs, and special events that are not tabulated by any statistical organization. *Ad Age* estimates these unmeasured expenditures.

In publishing this list of the 100 Leading National Advertisers, *Ad Age* includes salient information about each company in addition to its ad spending.

The 100 Leading National Advertisers List (1991 figures) included in 1992 four companies that spent over $1 billion:

Procter & Gamble Company	$2.149 billion
Philip Morris Companies	2.046 billion
General Motors Corporation	1.442 billion
Sears Roebuck & Company	1.179 billion

All 100 Leading National Advertisers spent $100 million a year or more on advertising. As a group, their total expenditure on advertising was $33.7 billion.

Some statistics about this select 100:

• Network TV gets the largest share of the top 100's spending, about $7.1 billion, or 76 percent of all U.S. advertising expenditures in this medium.

• The 100 Leading National Advertisers, as a group, spent big dollars on magazines—$2.79 billion—and on newspaper advertising—$1.51 billion.

• General Motors spent more on network TV advertising in 1991 than anyone else—almost $528 million.

• The largest advertiser in magazines is the number-three company in the top 100, General Motors. They bought $250 million worth of advertising in 1991.

• PepsiCo, the fifth-largest advertiser—$903 million—owns the Pizza Hut, Kentucky Fried Chicken (now known as KFC), and Taco Bell restaurant chains. To support the hearty appetite of these fast-food operations as well as the company's soft-drink business, PepsiCo is the largest advertiser on spot TV. Spot TV sales are commercial buys by an advertiser only in specific markets rather than in a whole network.

• In thirty-ninth place on the list is the U.S. government. It spent $253 million on advertising in 1991. The U.S. Army is the government's largest advertiser, with $50 million spent; the U.S. Postal Service is next, with $49 million; and the U.S. Navy is third, with $5 million. Eight ad agencies split all this government ad business. And—talk about client loyalty—J. Walter Thompson has had the U.S. Marine account since 1946.

Source: Reprinted with permission from *Advertising Age*, September 23, 1992, © Crain Communications, Inc. 1992.

TOTAL U.S. AD SPENDING BY CATEGORY AND MEDIA

The top two categories in terms of total ad spending are automotive and retail. The total for automotive was $5.259 billion; for retail, $5.126 billion. Here is an across-the-board look at these categories and where they spent their 1991 ad dollars:

	AUTOMOTIVE	RETAIL
	($ in millions)	
Magazine	$ 940	$ 197
Sunday magazines	38	93
Newspaper	746	2,492
Outdoor	52	63
Network TV	1,560	352
Spot TV	1,481	1,528
Syndicated TV	121	40
Cable TV	118	43
Network radio	72	92
Spot radio	132	226

Source: Reprinted with permission from *Advertising Age*, September 23, 1992, © Crain Communications, Inc. 1992.

Note the extensive use of television advertising by the automotive industry, representing about 60 percent of its total advertising expenditure. The retail industry is still the heavyweight advertiser in newspapers, accounting for almost 50 percent of all dollars spent in this medium. When retailers cut back on their spending in periods of economic slumps, newspapers suffer inordinately because advertising is their primary revenue source.

ADWEEK'S SUPERBRANDS

ADWEEK'S MARKETING WEEK publishes an annual SuperBrands Report. A superbrand is a marketer's, or advertiser's, core brand. It is a brand with global recognition and sales in the half-billion-to-multi-billion-dollar range. It is also the brand that receives a heavy advertising commitment. Here is a list of the ten most important brands—the superbrands in the world's and United States' markets:

WORLD	UNITED STATES
1. Coca-Cola	1. Coca-Cola
2. Sony	2. Campbell Soup
3. Mercedes-Benz	3. Disney
4. Kodak	4. Pepsi-Cola
5. Disney	5. Kodak
6. Nestlé	6. NBC
7. Toyota	7. Black & Decker
8. McDonald's	8. Kellogg
9. IBM	9. McDonald's
10. Pepsi-Cola	10. Hershey

It is interesting to note the world popularity of Coca-Cola, while powerful brands in the United States such as Campbell Soup, Black & Decker, Kellogg, and Hershey have yet to make their mark on the world's scene. With the democratization of Eastern Europe and the opening up of world markets generally, more American superbrands will gain fame globally.

For a greater understanding of superbrands, we have extracted from *ADWEEK*'s September 1992 listings the top brands in terms of sales in fourteen different classifications. We also give the brands' total annual sales and media expenditures:

CATEGORY	BRAND	TOTAL SALES	MEDIA EXPENDITURE (\$ in millions)
Athletic Footwear	Nike	\$4.9 billion	94
Family Sedans	Honda Accord	399,297 units	50
Beer	Budweiser	45.2 million barrels	105
Soft Drinks	Coca-Cola	2,522 million cases	150
Color Cosmetics	Cover Girl	\$406.6 million	61
Fast Food	McDonald's	\$12.5 billion	386

Top 40 Foods	Oscar Mayer	$2.5 billion	31
Cereals	Cheerios	$570 million	69
Soap	Dove	$165 million	19
Laundry Detergent	Tide	$997 million	62
Internal Analgesics	Tylenol	$605 million (wholesale sales)	71
Tobacco	Marlboro	$11.6 billion	100
Toys	Nintendo	$3.5 billion	45
Rental Cars	Hertz	$4.0 billion	44

What is significant about this list is the proportionate amount spent on advertising by various superbrands. Marlboro spends less than 1 percent of sales on advertising. In contrast, Procter & Gamble budgets 15 percent to advertise its Cover Girl cosmetic products.

Budweiser has the largest sales volume and spends the most on advertising to achieve its dominance of the beer market. Its sales are almost two and a half times that of the number-two brand, Miller Lite. McDonald's is clearly the Big Mac in the fast food business. It is truly a global brand. The company has sales two times higher than its number-two competitor, Burger King.

In the food business, the Oscar Mayer line of processed meats has annual sales of $2.5 billion. Number one on the cereals list is General Mills' Cheerios, with annual sales of $570 million, a very substantial figure.

As we can see, the dominant superbrands all spend heavily on advertising, yet this factor alone does not guarantee stardom. One key ingredient is certainly the sales and marketing clout of the product's parent company.

CHAPTER 17

A Profile of the Largest Advertiser in the United States

P rocter & Gamble (P&G) is one of the world's largest consumer packaged-goods companies. According to *Advertising Age*, in 1991 the parent company's sales reached $27 billion, with net earnings after taxes of $1.77 billion. P&G spent $1.166 billion on measured ad spending in 1991, edging its nearest competitor, Philip Morris, by $56 million.

The company is split into four major divisions, as listed, along with some of its representative brands:

PERSONAL CARE
(includes beauty care and health care)

Crest	Cover Girl
Head & Shoulders	Nyquil
Oil of Olay	Metamucil

LAUNDRY AND CLEANING

Tide	Cascade
Cheer	Ivory

FOOD AND BEVERAGE

Folger's coffee   Hawaiian Punch

Duncan Hines   Crisco

PULP AND CHEMICALS

Bounty   Luvs

Always   Charmin

HOW THE NATION'S LARGEST ADVERTISER SPENDS MORE THAN $1 BILLION A YEAR

In order to achieve its dominant position in the marketplace, P&G makes major commitments to advertising on behalf of its brands. Here are the company's eight top advertisers and their 1991 measured ad spending, according to *100 Leading National Advertisers/Advertising Age:*

	($ in millions)
Folgers coffee	$67,753
Tide laundry products	51,062
Crest toothpaste	44,784
Head & Shoulders shampoo	34,603
Nyquil cold products	31,929
Pampers diapers	29,151
Cheer laundry detergent	26,100
Downy fabric softener	25,425

Four of P&G's personal care products spend more than $25 million a year on advertising.

WHERE THE MONEY IS SPENT AND WHO DOES THE SPENDING

Seventeen advertising agencies are responsible for marketing the parent company's numerous brands. Network TV advertising in 1991 received the largest share of the company's $2.1 billion advertising expenditure, almost $516 million. About $143 million was spent in magazines and only $3.7 million in newspapers. The unusually large sum of $983 million went for unmeasured media—coupons, sampling, point of purchase.

Although account assignments are divided among the seventeen agencies, five receive the largest number of brands. Leo Burnett, based in Chicago, has Bold, Crest, Cheer, Lava, Luvs, Secret, Pert, Pepto-Bismol, Prell, and Noxzema. The agency's executive vice president–account director is the head person on the account.

D'Arcy Masius Benton & Bowles in New York has nineteen brands; Grey Advertising, based in New York, has ten P&G brands, Tatham/RSCG in Chicago has ten brands; and Saatchi & Saatchi in New York, nine brands. At each of these agencies a senior vice president or executive vice president has overall responsibility for P&G's products.

At the corporate level at P&G, each division and product group has a group vice president and vice president/general manager supervising the advertising and marketing of a number of brands. That individual is responsible for planning, marketing research, and promotion. However, the day-to-day liaison with the agency is conducted by each brand's product manager.

PROCTER & GAMBLE AS A GLOBAL MARKETER

As with other major U.S. packaged-goods companies, P&G is broadening its international scope. Business outside the United States represented fully 46 percent of its total sales in 1991. Its brands are now marketed in more than 140 countries. For example, its Vidal Sassoon brand is now Europe's best-selling shampoo, and Oil of Olay is the top facial moisturizer in Europe.

For multilingual people with a marketing bent, a career with Procter & Gamble may be a passport to success.

CHAPTER 18

Companies That Handle Their Advertising Internally

We have written about the function of advertising within agencies and in client-advertisers. There are also advertising jobs within companies that choose to prepare and place their own advertising, thereby bypassing the use of advertising agencies.

These companies set up "house agencies." They do this for two basic reasons: First, they are able to maintain greater control of their advertising; also, they are often able to save money. For example, if an agency places an ad in a magazine for $10,000, it receives a commission from the publication of 15 percent, or $1,500. When an advertiser has established a house agency and places the same $10,000 ad, the advertiser will receive the $1,500 commission itself.

Yet even though a company may save money on its advertising expenditures, it still must concern itself with the media selection and creative aspects of advertising. Here, too, the company has options. It may employ this talent in-house or use outside specialist firms.

This can be a problem, particularly for a large advertiser. At an ad agency, the client receives the combined talent of many individuals and departments. The client's media selection is reviewed by a top media executive. If the account is a large one, a creative director oversees the preparation of copy and art. And, finally, an account supervisor or account executive will tend to all the client's advertising needs on a daily basis.

Of course, if an advertiser is willing to pay for them, all of these services may be purchased from outside specialists or performed by in-house staff.

The Standard Directory of Advertising Agencies lists hundreds of house agency operations. Substantial companies, such as Olivetti, Dana Perfumes, Jordache, La Choy Food Products, Jantzen, Lands' End, Munsingwear, Wella shampoo, The Gap, Amerada Hess, Grolier Enterprises, and Calvin Klein handle their advertising through house agencies.

The Calvin Klein apparel interests place about $12 million a year in TV advertising and $8 million in magazine advertising. They accomplish this with a director of administration, a creative director, a production director, and only seven other employees in the marketing division.

Hart Services in Chicago is the house agency for the large men's apparel organization Hart Schaffner & Marx. With only thirty-two employees, the agency places $15 million in billings for a variety of brands.

The John F. Murray Advertising Company in New York, established in 1912, places $240 million in TV advertising and $35 million in magazines for its parent, the giant American Home Products Company. Their staff numbers only thirty-five employees. However, the Murray agency's primary function is purchasing network TV advertising; other functions, such as creative and production, are done by six or seven outside agencies.

WHAT KINDS OF ADVERTISERS
USE IN-HOUSE ADVERTISING STAFFS?

A department store in a city with a population of 200,000 that spends $250,000 a year on local advertising will often choose to prepare and place its own advertising. Basically, this may include ads in local newspapers and in "shoppers." These are mailing pieces distributed or marketed to a store's customer or prospect list.

An in-house department such as this one will often have its own desktop publishing equipment to facilitate the typesetting of these ads. Operating this equipment requires special training.

The department store handling its own advertising will also need a copywriter, an art director, and an individual trained to purchase advertising. Of these, the copywriting job is the most important, since it involves the creation of provocative copy that is used in ads for sales and other promotions.

Generally speaking, ad jobs such as these are not considered as prestigious as those in an ad agency or jobs for an advertiser that employs an ad agency. Salaries for in-house ad departments are typically low, about equal to those in small ad agencies. The principal benefit in taking these jobs is in gaining experience in the advertising process. In many cases, the individual working at an in-house advertising job is a one-person advertising staff. In this capacity one learns the discipline of meeting deadlines. He or she may also be called upon to write and edit copy, lay out artwork, and select and evaluate media. Also, an in-house ad job often offers the opportunity of working right in your own hometown.

What kind of jobs are available at in-house ad departments? Here is a rundown:

CREATIVE. A copywriter creates the concept of ads and actually writes the copy. If TV and radio are used, the copywriter creates the commercials and works with outside sources on their execution.

An art director and his or her assistants make layouts for print ads and, using desktop publishing techniques or mechanical pasteup, prepare the advertising. The art director also works on the preparation of TV and radio commercials. In addition to working on ad preparation, both the copywriter and art director are responsible for brochures, booklets, and other promotional material.

MEDIA. If the in-house ad department places advertising in a variety of media, a media planner/buyer evaluates these sources and then actually places orders for this advertising.

PRODUCTION. A production manager traffics the ad department's output through its various phases. He or she also deals with printers, typesetters, and other outside suppliers on the company's advertising and collateral material.

Directing these in-house departments is usually the responsibility of an advertising director or manager. The number of people under his or her direction depends on the volume of advertising placed by the company.

PART IV

Pursuing a Career in Advertising

CHAPTER 19

Education, Preparation, and Resources

A dvertising offers an interesting and often dynamic career to the increasing numbers of talented and creative young people who turn to it each year. It is a challenging industry that seeks people with initiative, imagination, and sound judgment coupled with an understanding of communications and business. For those with ability and determination, the rewards are great.

STUDENT INTERNSHIPS

Advertising is a popular career choice for both job seekers and career changers. Its reputation as a glamour field attracts many who are highly qualified. Education, especially with a major in advertising or marketing, or an M.B.A. degree, will certainly open doors. Internship programs, maintained by some agencies and advertisers, provide additional entrée. Unfortunately, there is no listing available of which agencies and advertisers have such programs. But here are a few suggestions:

1. Visit a library that has copies of *The Standard Advertising Register,* which lists major advertiser companies, and *The Standard Directory of Advertising Agencies.* Choose an agency or advertiser located in the city of your choice and write to the director of human resources to ask if the agency has an internship program and how it works. As a general rule, the larger the company, the better your chances.

2. Find out if the company has an on-site internship supervisor. It is an important asset to a company's program.

3. If you are in college and your school has such a program, a good time to do your internship is between your sophomore and junior year or during your junior year.

4. You must send a résumé and cover letter to apply for an internship. Follow the same procedure you would if you were applying for a regular job. (See page 145 for a sample résumé and Chapter 25 for tips from an expert.)

5. Often an interview is required for internships. Consider the interview as a major opportunity. Ask questions. Discuss your duties. Follow up the interview with a thank-you letter. A large agency or corporation will pay interns, but it may be wise for you to apply at a smaller company at no pay if the chances are better for a full-time job after graduation.

The American Association of Advertising Agencies (AAAA), 666 Third Avenue, New York, NY 10017, offers twenty-five salaried ten-week summer jobs in New York and Chicago for minority college students. Write for full information.

EMPLOYMENT AGENCIES

Most employment agencies and headhunters (executive recruiters) specializing in advertising do not handle entry-level jobs. However, it is worth investigating the employment agencies in your city to find out their policies. Call these employment agencies to determine whether they do a lot of business with ad agencies.

There are two employment agencies in New York City that specialize in advertising personnel: the Judy Wald Agency, Inc., 210 East Sixtieth Street, New York, NY 10022; and Jerry Fields Associates, Inc., 353 Lexington Avenue, New York, NY 10016. Fields is an affiliate of the Howard-Sloan-Koller Group, a major recruiter for the media industry. The Wald and Fields agencies operate coast to coast. Their fees, usually paid by the employer, run from 15 percent to 30 percent of the employee's first year's salary. In some cases, agencies or client companies will pay part or all of the employee's relocation expenses.

There are three other recruiting firms in New York that specialize in advertising. The Gumbinner Company deals with account service people; Susan Friedman Ltd. specializes in creative executive recruitment and consulting; and Simmy Sussman, a search and consulting firm, handles media executive placement.

Most cities with a reasonable number of ad agencies have ad clubs. Find out the name of the club in your own city or in the city in which you are seeking employment. The club director will surely know the names of that city's employment agencies specializing in advertising. Often these clubs have set up job clearinghouse services or vocational-guidance committees that may be helpful in locating a job.

SCHOOLS

There are more than a hundred U.S. colleges and universities offering courses in marketing and advertising, and many of them offer majors in these subjects as well. An excellent booklet detailing these programs, *Where Shall I Go to College to Study Advertising?*, may be obtained by sending $2.00 to Advertising Education Publications, 623 Meadow Bend Drive, Baton Rouge, LA 70808.

For information about college courses and internships that may be available in your area, contact the American Advertising Federation, Educational Services Dept., 1400 K Street, N.W., Suite 1000, Washington, DC 20005.

The School of Visual Arts

New York City has many fine academic institutions for undergraduate studies and continuing education. None, however, can match the School of Visual Arts (SVA) in the depth of its concentration in the media arts.

There are about twenty-two hundred full-time undergraduate students who are taught by 650 faculty members, all working professionals. Also, four thousand students attend the continuing-education program.

The school has an in-house design studio that produces award-winning books, booklets, magazines, ads, and films. The Public Advertising System of the SVA is a media arts department course that functions like an advertising agency. Students develop ad campaigns, brochures, posters, and TV commercials for public-service clients such as the President's Committee on Employment of the Handicapped, the New York City Department of Health, Planned Parenthood, and the Sickle Cell Disease Foundation.

There are ten areas of specialization within the SVA's curriculum. Each discipline has its first-through-fourth-year requirements, with a liberal sprinkling of electives to widen the scope of the specialization. Three such disciplines applicable to this book are as follows:

1. Film and video: New York attracts many of the best writers, producers, directors, and editors. Professionals who work in commercial filmmaking, video and broadcasting, and advertising production serve as faculty for students in this specialty. Some representative courses include Introduction to Videotape, Writing as Communications, Film Production, Advanced Editing, Advanced Cinematography, and Documentary Video.

2. Media arts: The specialty of media arts encompasses graphic design and art direction, account management, media planning, and print and broadcast copywriting.

3. Communication arts: In the glamorous world of print, broadcast journalism, and public relations, New York is the international hub. Students in this specialty benefit from the introduction of local professionals in radio, TV, and newspapers. There is an eight-semester humanities core program intermixed with specialist courses in film, photography, and journalism.

SVA also maintains a strong continuing-education program. The school's motto "When the job you have is not enough, but the job you want is out of reach" conveys the thrust of the SVA's visual arts continuing-education program. Go there, they say, when you're between jobs, and go there at night and on Saturdays while you're working and want to prepare for a new career.

Here is just a sprinkling of the evening and weekend courses in media arts and advertising offered at the SVA in 1992:

> Magazine Design Portfolio
> Creating Television and Movie Posters
> Magazine Design
> Principles of Pharmaceutical Advertising
> Producing a Commercial Spot
> Advertising for People Who Are Already in Advertising
> The Best Writers Are Good Art Directors—
>   The Best Art Directors Are Good Writers

The average cost of a course in continuing education at the SVA is $270. For further information, write to School of Visual Arts, 209 East Twenty-third Street, New York, NY 10010.

Other Programs

There are a number of other outstanding schools offering programs in graphic design. These include Cooper Union and Parsons School of Design in New York City, Pratt Institute in Brooklyn, the Art Center College of Design in Pasadena, California, and the Philadelphia College of Art and the Moore College of Art in Philadelphia.

ORGANIZATIONS

The American Advertising Federation's College Chapters

The American Advertising Federation (AAF) is the only national advertising association encompassing and representing all aspects and disciplines of the advertising industry. Its membership includes four hundred companies, two hundred ad clubs, and twenty-five thousand individuals, along with 175 college chapters with more than forty-five hundred members.

The AAF's primary objectives for their college chapters are "to encourage young people to enter advertising as a career and to enhance the quality of advertising education." Its annual National Student Advertising Competition challenges student teams to take the advertising/marketing case study of a national company and develop a marketing plan, advertising campaign, and media strategy to meet specified challenges and goals.

The 1990 competition, sponsored by American Airlines, challenged students in over two hundred colleges and universities nationwide to complete an unusual assignment. American provided AAF students an insight into the airline industry and asked them to analyze and recommend a detailed communications plan to position American Airlines as the premier U.S. flag carrier in the world. Previous National Student Advertising Competition sponsors have included Nabisco, Coca-Cola, Burger King, Chevrolet Motor Division, and the Hearst Corporation. In 1991 the sponsor of the competition was Visa.

The Advertising Research Foundation

The principal mission of the Advertising Research Foundation (ARF) is "to develop and maintain a continuing program of activities and publications designed to serve the industry by advancing the state of the art of advertising, marketing, and media research." Its membership comes from advertising agencies as well as advertisers. The ARF conducts conferences and workshops and publishes more than thirty publications yearly and a management newsletter. About thirty-five colleges are ARF members.

Readers interested in advertising research should contact the ARF regarding its various programs. Its address is Advertising Research Foundation, 3 East Fifty-fourth Street, New York, NY 10022.

THE JOB OUTLOOK—AN APPRAISAL

One needs to be realistic and objective about the employment opportunities in advertising and marketing. At this writing, when the nation's economy is feeling the effects of a recessionary period, jobs in this glamour field do not abound. Corporations have cut back on their advertising budgets, and, commensurately, agencies have cut staff instead of hiring new people. But economic conditions are cyclical; a rebound can quickly follow a downturn, and active hiring may resume.

The poor job market does not appear to have affected the number of college students majoring in advertising. At Syracuse University, enrollment in this field doubled during the 1980s, as it did at the University of Texas. At Michigan State, one of the largest ad schools in the country with fourteen hundred ad majors, administrators have had to turn people away. The coordinator of the advertising program at California State University at Fullerton, with eleven hundred advertising majors, states, "The job market isn't good. But that doesn't seem to be discouraging anyone."

Some students have attacked the problem realistically by seeking internships and employment abroad. A ray of hope comes from Allen Rosenshine, head of the giant advertising agency BBDO Worldwide. "As advertising becomes more global, there's going to be a need for trained people, but not necessarily in local markets. I don't know how you can look at the current state of world events and think anything else."

PUBLICATIONS

Career Booklets
Two valuable advertising career booklets are available: *Advertising: A Guide to Careers in Advertising* (single copy $2.00 postpaid) is available from the American Association of Advertising Agencies, Inc., 666 Third Avenue, New York, NY 10017. *Jobs in Advertising* (send 75 cents per copy and a self-addressed stamped envelope) is available from the Bureau of Education and Research, American Advertising Federation, 1400 K Street, N.W., Washington, DC 20005.

The Two Most Important Advertising/Marketing Magazines

Want a quick education in marketing without ever taking a college course? Just subscribe to *Advertising Age* and *ADWEEK*. If you can't afford it, find a library that files them. You'll sound like an industry pro in a year and be able to "run it up the flagpole" with the best of them. Along with their dozens of news and feature pieces, both have good want-ad sections for jobs in advertising. Let's take a brief look at each publication.

ADVERTISING AGE. *Ad Age,* as those in the industry call it, has been around for sixty-three years. It is published weekly and contains news, industry analysis, and articles on the fields of marketing, advertising, promotion, direct mail, media buying, research, retailing, and brand management, all delivered in an authoritative yet concise style.

Emphasizing the global nature of advertising and marketing today, *Ad Age International,* a special news supplement, is published monthly and bound inside *Ad Age.* In some major overseas cities, *Ad Age International* is delivered on the Monday of issue date just as it is in the United States.

A standard feature of *Ad Age* is its yearly publication of forty-eight in-depth special reports. In 1993, for example, *Ad Age*'s special reports are tackling such subjects as data base marketing, entertainment marketing, environmental marketing, television syndication, marketing to teens, technology in the ad agency, cable TV, and computer marketing. The three most important special issues *Ad Age* puts out each year are *100 Leading Media Companies, 100 Leading National Advertisers,* and *The Agency Report,* in which it names an "Agency of the Year." And, for what many agency people use as ammunition for salary increases, *Ad Age* publishes an annual salary survey.

Ad Age's *100 Leading Advertisers* issue demonstrates the publication's outstanding research capabilities. In this issue, for each of the 100 leading advertisers there is information on where it spends its budget; the sales and earnings of each of the company's divisions; and a list of its personnel and brands and their agencies. Accompanying this report is a corporate profile that details the company's progress during the previous year in terms of market share, new product launches, and objectives. Agency executives, of course, use this information for leads on potential new accounts. The media uses it as well, to find out where advertisers are spending their money. For example, a TV network might seek out an advertiser's brand that is spending more on print ads and less in broadcast.

Ad Age publishes three regional editions—Eastern, Central, and Western—so that editorial emphasis may be keyed in to these areas and advertisers are able to focus their advertising for maximum effectiveness.

Ad Age leads its competitor, *ADWEEK*, in circulation and ad dollars. As of early 1993, the paid circulation of *Ad Age* was over eighty-five thousand and the magazine was selling over $25 million in advertising annually. A subscription to *Ad Age* is $86 for fifty-two issues. Write to *Advertising Age*, Circulation Department, 965 East Jefferson Avenue, Detroit, MI 48207-3185.

Creativity, an editorial outgrowth of *Ad Age*, is a monthly publication for the advertising and marketing creative community. Each issue of *Creativity* is sent to more than 30,000 qualified ad agency creative and production people. Its editorial coverage includes analyses of ads and creative campaigns, trends, and profiles of creative front-runners. One regular feature is "Desktop Creativity," spotlighting innovations in this dynamic technology.

Ad Age also conducts conferences, often cosponsored by other organizations, and produces training videos for its recently launched Ad Age Video Library.

ADWEEK. In 1981, before *ADWEEK* was so named by its new owners, the publication was composed of three regional advertising magazines with the funky titles *Anny* (Advertising News of New York), *Sam* (Serving Advertisers in the Midwest), and *Mac* (Media Advertisers and Clients).

The *ADWEEK* network today is composed of six regional editions: New England, East, West, Midwest, Southeast, and Southwest. If you subscribe to *ADWEEK* and live in Los Angeles, for example, you receive a copy of the western edition every week. That means your issue will contain a cover and twelve to sixteen pages of the western edition with its own coverage of the local advertising scene wrapped around the standard body of *ADWEEK*.

ADWEEK is edited for the fast-changing agency business and the creative scene. Its editorial slant is breezy yet informative. In terms of format, *ADWEEK* is the traditional 8¼-by-11-inch size, while its competitor, *Ad Age*, is 11 by 14¼ inches.

ADWEEK publishes about forty special reports a year that are bound into the publication. Some subjects the magazine tackled in 1992 were the domestic auto market, marketing for children, fast foods, cosmetics, Hispanic marketing, and travel. *ADWEEK*'s special reports also include two widely read annual articles, "The 10 Hottest Magazines" and "The Agency Report Card."

ADWEEK's paid circulation is about fifty-two thousand. A subscription is $89 for fifty-one weekly issues. Write to *ADWEEK*, Subscriber Service Center, P.O. Box 700, Brewster, NY 10509-9942.

The *ADWEEK* people also publish *BRANDWEEK,* formerly known as *ADWEEK's Marketing Week.* Its editorial emphasis is on advertisers and the brand-name products and services they bring to market. Editorial coverage includes news, case histories of new product launches, marketing strategies, legislation, and trends. *BRANDWEEK* runs a large number of special reports on subjects similar to those in *ADWEEK.* However, its thrust is the marketing aspect of these subject areas. *BRANDWEEK* has a paid circulation of about twelve thousand and a qualified unpaid circulation of about fourteen thousand. A subscription is $85 for fifty-one weekly issues. Write to *BRANDWEEK,* Subscriber Service Center, P.O. Box 701, Brewster, NY 10509-9988.

A third magazine from *ADWEEK* is *MEDIAWEEK,* formerly known as *Marketing & Media Decisions* under its previous ownership. *AD-WEEK* launched the magazine in early 1991. *MEDIAWEEK* is edited for the interest of media planners, buyers, supervisors, and other professionals involved in the puchase of media. It covers "avails" (special media opportunities available), pricing, trends, and news. *MEDIAWEEK* is also active on the special reports front. It publishes about forty of these a year, dealing with its own special interests. Some special reports, such as "The 10 Hottest Magazines," appear in all three of these *ADWEEK* publications.

MEDIAWEEK has a paid circulation of about three thousand and a qualified unpaid circulation of sixteen thousand. The cost of a subscription is $75 for fifty-one weekly issues. Write to *MEDIAWEEK,* Subscriber Service Center, P.O. Box 708, Brewster, NY 10509-9905.

An important adjunct to *ADWEEK*'s business is its seminars and conferences. About six of these are conducted each year at various locations. They run for three days and are divided into as many as forty different two- and three-hour sessions, led by experienced industry professionals. The diversity of subject matter makes these seminars attractive to experienced agency and marketing people as well as beginners. A single two-hour seminar costs about $75.

Other Publications Related to Advertising

The people at Cowles Business Media publish two excellent magazines for the publishing industry: *Folio:* and *Publishing News*. Recently they have come out with a sprightly newcomer, *Inside Media,* which covers advertising as well as the broadcasting and publishing media. A one-year subscription (twenty-four issues) is $49. Write to *Inside Media,* Six River Bend, Box 4272, Stamford, CT 06907. It is also available in some libraries. Its direction is "inside," but it is nevertheless informative. As they say in the book business, a must read.

There are a number of other publications dealing with some phase of advertising. They include *Art Direction, Body Copy, Direct Marketing Magazine, International Advertiser, Journal of Marketing,* and *Marketing News.* Some are available in libraries.

CONFERENCES AND SEMINARS

Both *ADWEEK* and *Ad Age* produce additional revenues for their operations by staging conferences. *Ad Age* conducts a Creative Workshop each summer for four days where "creatives" from agencies and advertisers attend classes and symposia on creative marketing strategy and advertising execution. About forty lecturers from the client and agency side address the group on a variety of subjects.

In addition to being a learning experience, these seminars offer not only useful information but also an excellent opportunity to make contacts. For example, an account executive from a Los Angeles agency might attend a lecture by the vice president, marketing services, of Procter & Gamble on "The Importance of Brand Franchise Building." At the same time, the account executive has the chance to question the lecturer about jobs at P&G; he or she may have lunch with a lecture classmate who is an agency head from Denver.

Conferences such as *Ad Age*'s Creative Workshop are expensive. Including meals and hotel and the cost of the session, the four-day tab may run to about $2,000.

For *Ad Age,* the conference is a profit center. It is also good image building, since it establishes the publication as an industry leader concerned with the dissemination of information and ideas.

ADWEEK is also a heavyweight in the seminar business, conducting three- or four-day regional conferences. Their seminars are geared to the experienced professional who needs the latest information and state-of-the-art techniques as well as to the newcomer to the field eager to learn everything.

ADWEEK's seminars may be attended as individual sessions or on a one-, two-, or three-day basis. Since this attendance has a legitimate professional educational purpose, it is deemed to be tax-deductible.

CHAPTER 20

Getting the Job

E ach year the New York office of a large international agency receives more than ten thousand inquiries for entry-level jobs. The firm hires only *forty* new people. Even so, agencies complain of a talent gap in their creative departments. The problem is not the number of bodies but the shortage of creative stars.

As one senior creative director put it, "We've never had a shortage of candidates. Plenty of young people have come to us over the years wanting to be copywriters or art directors, but the problem traditionally has been finding the really terrific ones who can make a difference."

One thirty-year-old superstar-copywriter with eight years' experience makes well over $100,000 at a large New York packaged-goods agency. He has already held four different jobs and claims to get five offers a week to jump to another agency, with each agency offering a tempting compensation package.

Lintas has published a fine booklet called "The Determined Person's Guide to Getting a Job in Advertising." To obtain a free copy, write to:

> Patricia A. Ransom, Vice President–Personnel Manager
> Lintas: New York
> One Dag Hammarskjold Plaza
> New York, NY 10017

CAREER TIP

If you're applying for a job either as an artist or a copywriter, a portfolio is very important. A portfolio is also called a book. Books, or portfolios, are scrapbooks of the work you have done on print ads or radio and TV commercials. If you have been involved in creating film commercials, you will collect these on a reel. You will also include in your portfolio the storyboards from which these commercials were created. Storyboards are frame-by-frame visuals and the accompanying copy for commercials.

Since advertising is a collaborative effort, you should be honest in your résumé and portfolio about the role you played in creating these ads.

What if you are applying for an entry-level position and have no art or writing credits? Some people clip ads from magazines and redesign or rewrite them. Others create new campaigns for real products or services. One ad veteran advises beginners to invent situations that require advertising and to create advertising for them.

You can develop a portfolio by working for an advertiser, such as a department store or a manufacturer. Schools like New York's School of Visual Arts stress preparation of a portfolio. Concentrate on print advertising in your portfolio. Try to include a campaign rather than single ads. Communicate your ability to create campaign themes. Make sure the portfolio is neat and well organized and keep the copy within readable limits.

Get advice from experts about how to put together a portfolio. It is your most important calling card.

Many books describe the job-hunting process. One of the best, geared specifically for advertising jobs, is the booklet prepared by the American Association of Advertising Agencies (AAAA), "Go For It—A Guide to Careers in Advertising." It breaks down the job hunt into the following phases:

1. *Educate yourself about the business.* Read everything you can find about advertising. Most college and other libraries will have a collection of books on advertising and marketing (see Recommended Reading, page 183). Read the important trade publications in this field (see chapter 19). A year's back issues of three or four of these publications will contain a wealth of information about agencies, ad campaigns, and trends in the advertising business.

2. *Network.* Talk to people who are in the field. Learn from professionals where your talents and interests will best serve the industry. The networking process snowballs very quickly—the more you do it, the easier it is.

3. *Visit the local advertising club.* Most cities with fifteen or more ad agencies will have an advertising club. These are excellent places to make contacts. Find out about the seminars they conduct and attend them. Many clubs post jobs available, and some will offer free situations-wanted ads in their newsletters. Make inquiries at such professional organizations as the AAAA and the American Advertising Federation.

4. *Target your prospects.* Never mind the low hiring rate of major agencies. Decide for yourself whom you want to work for. Examine a current copy of the Agency Red Book, formally known as the *Standard Directory of Advertising Agencies.* It lists thirty-five hundred agencies throughout this country and abroad, their account list, total billings, specialization, etc. It also lists the names and titles of key personnel. If a particular agency specializes in packaged goods and you already know this is a good place for you to be, target your effort on this agency. Read the trade press for other tips that will help you pinpoint the agency you want to work for.

5. *Develop a strategy.* "Unique selling proposition" (USP) is the basic premise of all good advertising. It is the way advertising makes the ideal connection between the product or service and the prospect. If executed properly, it becomes the "big enduring idea." That is, the advertising idea that the client may hang its marketing hat on for many years. Develop your own USP. Sell yourself to a prospective employer the way you would if you were writing an ad for a major campaign. Remember, your competition for agency and advertiser jobs may have even a stronger academic background than you have. Try something daring that shows your commitment, imagination, and analytic thinking—maybe a "new business approach" to an account that the agency doesn't currently have.

6. *Create a good résumé.* Dozens of books have been written about how to write a résumé. Read some. The sample on page 145 shows one format and exhibits the principles you should follow: Highlight your relevant skills. Reflect your talents, interests, and the benefits you will bring to the potential employer. Keep it neat, clear, precise, and all on one page. Tailor your résumé to each position you apply for. Don't waste space on clubs you belonged to in high school. Punctuation, spelling, and production of the résumé must be perfect.

7. *Take pains with each cover letter.* Don't blow the impact of a good résumé with a bad cover letter. Together they create a first impression of you. Stay clear of the form letter. Let them know why you're interested and why you think you're right for them. Pay special attention to spelling, typos, and grammar. Cover letters should be short. Say just what you want—*an interview.*

8. *Assemble a portfolio.* To land a job in an agency's creative department, you'll need a portfolio. (See page 140 for a description of the elements of a portfolio.) If you wrote ads for a local department store and they're good, submit them. If you're an aspiring art director, include ample demonstration of your design ability and graphic sense. If you're a budding copywriter, show examples of your work. Portfolio ads can be class projects, independent work, or actual ads. A good book on putting together a portfolio is *How to Put Your Book Together and Get a Job in Advertising* by Maxine Paetro (Dutton, 1980).

9. *Prepare for your interview.* If you are in school and you have a good placement department, find out if they can set up some role-playing situations with specific advice on handling an interview. Just getting an interview is a foot in the door. Once you've secured an interview, prepare for it carefully. Organize your thinking and review the information you have on the agency. Be articulate, self-confident, and enthusiastic. Talk about yourself—what you've learned, what you offer, and what you can do for Company X. Don't try to recite everything you know. Selectivity shows you are thinking.

The well-known media specialist Roger Bumstead contributes these additional thoughts on what "turns him off" in an interview:

> Candidates without a career focus . . . candidates who want me to do the talking . . . candidates who "laze" in the chair across from me . . . candidates who are either boring or arrogant . . . candidates who don't dress properly because they think it doesn't matter when they're seeing a recruiter. Wow, are they wrong!

Your appearance is all-important. Your clothing may have been bought at Sears or Penney's but it can and should look like it came from Brooks Brothers or Alcott & Andrews. We call it "the Corporate Look."

One last point about interviews. Within twenty-four hours after an interview, send your interviewer a follow-up letter. This is an excellent oppportunity to reiterate your interest in the position and express your appreciation for his or her time.

TIPS ON BREAKING INTO ADVERTISING

By now you may have a passionate eagerness to make it in advertising. We hope so, but it's not going to be easy. Here are specific tips to help you in your pursuit of fame and fortune in the advertising world.

• If recruiters from ad agencies visit your campus, be sure to attend. Ask questions and try to learn their hiring practices, interview systems, attitudes about requirements for graduate work, and so forth.

• Advertising is a young people's business. You may be over the hill by the time you're forty-five; nevertheless, I know a copywriter at a top-three agency who spent almost forty years with the company, never made it to top management, earned an excellent salary, and feels that he has had a very fulfilling career.

• Use friends or any contacts you can make to get an agency interview, preferably with an executive in the department that interests you. If a family member has a contact at a major advertiser, use it to get an interview with the agency.

• Consider any agency entry-level job, even secretarial. There you can learn by just being around advertising.

• If you live in a large city, take an evening course in advertising and marketing taught by professionals at one of the city's colleges.

• Read every book you can find about advertising. Subscribe to *Advertising Age, ADWEEK,* and *MEDIAWEEK.* If you can't afford a subscription, most college libraries and good local libraries have these publications on file.

• The top 100 agencies have about fifty thousand employees. If you choose to work for a small agency, note that salaries can be 20–50 percent less.

330 New Park Avenue
Anytown, NJ 07771
(201) 555-7531

September 25, 1992

Ms. Iris Forbes
Vice President, Human Resources
PRS Advertising
950 Third Avenue
New York, NY 10023

Dear Ms. Forbes:

As my enclosed résumé indicates, I am a recent management and communications graduate of Regis College. My experience includes various internships in the field of marketing.

I would like to meet with you in person regarding a job in account management and will call on Monday, October 5th, so that we may arrange a suitable date for an interview.

I look forward to meeting you.

Sincerely,

Christina M. Sherover

Enclosure

CHRISTINA M. SHEROVER
330 New Park Avenue
Anytown, NJ 07771
(201) 555-7531

OBJECTIVE: To obtain employment with an advertising/marketing agency or consumer products corporation, allowing me to utilize my marketing and communication skills and background.

EDUCATION: B.A. Management and Communications; Regis College, Weston, MA
Related courses in Marketing Principles, Human Resource Management, Computer Programming, Graphic Arts, Writing for the Media, Administrative Theory, and Public Relations.

EXPERIENCE: *American Tourister*, Marketing and Communications Department:
Warren, RI
Internship, January through May 1992
Expanded theory into practical application in both sales forecasting and demographics. Aided the Marketing Communications Manager in writing press releases, feature sheets, and new product information. Wrote reviews and recommendations for advertising scheduling in print media placement.

WJAR-TV: Providence, RI
Internship, May through December 1991
Assistant in the news department. Conducted research, monitored competitive network stations, assisted reporters on field assignments, and participated in promotional commercials.
From May through August, averaged at least 20 hours weekly.
While attending college, averaged 8 hours weekly.

Merchandising and Marketing Corporation: Dobbs Ferry, NY
Marketing assistant, August 25 through September 13, 1991
Aided at an international marketing conference in Paris, France, with representatives from 18 different countries. Planned and organized material for presentations, assisted in same, and processed requests for samples.

December 1990 through January 1991
Researched promotional material, organized same, and then assisted in the sales presentations to several clients. This New York–based marketing company's clients include major consumer-products companies in food, beverage, drug, liquor, soft goods, and other industries.

Internship, December 1989 through January 1990
Participated in the implementation of new promotions, improved office promotional premium file system, and assisted in sales presentations.

May through September 1989
Developed promotional ideas with a new client, served as production assistant, organized office system, and assisted in sales presentations and general clerical work.

Professional references available.

• New York agencies are not keen on transfers from agencies in smaller cities because of different work style and pace. But if you come from a client, say, Procter & Gamble in Cincinnati, that's another story. They are an outstanding packaged-goods training ground.

• Before you go to work for an agency, find out about its training program. Many don't have this important feature.

• If you're interested in advertising and marketing but don't want to work in New York or in an ad agency, consider employment at a major advertiser like Philip Morris, which has divisions all over the country. They spend $2 billion a year on advertising. If you become a product or brand manager, you will be responsible for all phases of a product's marketing, including test marketing, product development, advertising campaign, packaging, and so on. It's a challenging, well-paid job.

• If you want to go into account management at an ad agency, you should think seriously about getting an M.B.A. You'll have a better chance to get that important first job, and you'll earn much more money to start. Also, product managers who work most closely with account executives are often M.B.A.s. They prefer working with other M.B.A.s so they can talk "M.B.A.-speak."

• When you get an agency job—whether account management, media, or creative—learn all you can about a client's business. Read the annual report and marketing literature. Study the competition and the trade practices in the industry.

• Marketing and advertising jobs with advertisers are more stable than account-executive jobs at agencies. At an advertiser, if you perform well and the company is not sold, you're not at risk.

GETTING AN AD JOB IN POOR ECONOMIC TIMES

Ad agencies traditionally use an employment ratio of a certain number of people per $1 million in billings. When the economy is weak and clients cut their ad spending, agencies reduce this ratio—in some cases to as low as one or two people per $1 million in ad billings. In a recessionary climate, the generalist has the best chance of surviving. Stretch your horizons. If your entry-level employment trained you for one specialty, learn all you can about others. An assistant account executive with a good working knowledge of media buying is more valuable to an agency than an account executive without additional experience.

If you are at the entry level, take any ad job you can find, client or agency. Be prepared to move to a less glamorous city than the large one of your choice.

Accept a lesser paying job than you expect, especially if it increases your broad knowledge of the whole field.

Take the courses necessary to become bilingual. With this knowledge, you may qualify for an ad-agency job abroad. This is especially possible if you have some solid advertising experience.

If you have a sales personality, consider an entry-level job in your city selling yellow pages advertising. You will learn a great deal about small business, further your selling skills, and in some cases learn to create the advertising itself—all good experience for your future career.

Read all the industry trade publications. They often have help-wanted sections. A recent West Coast edition of *MEDIAWEEK* had five pages of these ads.

And, finally, use networking to widen your scope and increase your job sources.

CHAPTER 21

Ad-Agency Training Programs

A lthough it's difficult to get *any* job at an ad agency, find out if the agency you are applying to has a training program. It is worth the extra effort to try to get a job at an agency that has a tradition of training, such as Ogilvy & Mather Worldwide or Leo Burnett. There may be a big expense in such training programs, but agencies find it profitable in the long run. It is their way of discovering and nurturing bright young stars. Here are highlights from some of these programs.

OGILVY & MATHER WORLDWIDE

This giant agency, with eight thousand employees in 278 offices around the world, runs one of the most sophisticated training programs in the business. A senior vice president directs its worldwide training programs. Each of the specialized agencies, Ogilvy & Mather Direct, O&M Public Relations, and O&M Promotions, has its own training program, as does the parent agency. Specialty departments within each agency division—media, research, and so on—run their own programs. Local offices do their own training. In 1991, the senior vice president in charge of training conducted thirteen international training programs on various topics and disciplines. The program's objective: the training and development of about 250 supervisor-level stars—people already identified as outstanding employees.

The program director also assists sixty-five of their largest local offices in "in-house training" programs of their own. A local "in-house training director" runs this effort. All these training directors are given the excellent O&M training book, *A Guide to Effective In-House Training*. It even has tips on potential pitfalls, such as "avoid canned presentations."

The parent company also publishes a quarterly publication, *Let's Talk Training*, distributed to all 250 offices worldwide. O&M's training program is what college courses and books on advertising should be but often fall short of. O&M's New York media department has about 250 people. They prefer to hire at entry level: "Young, enthusiastic people . . . people who are involved, who are aggressive to an extent, have an open mind, have a good personality, enjoy themselves," says Executive Vice President/U.S. Media Director Larry Cole.

MCCANN-ERICKSON WORLDWIDE

This large agency runs a media training program curriculum for all new media-department employees. The program runs for five months and consists of two-hour lunchtime classes once a week. The "professors" are top executives in the media area. About twenty to twenty-five "students" take part in the program. As a final exam the students must put together a complete media plan for a McCann-Erickson client. There are no grades, but there is a diploma awarded at a McCann Media University cocktail party. Some of the subjects: computer basics, elementary media writing, national TV, and the last of the twenty-two session sequence of courses—critique of a media plan.

Ira Carlin, executive vice president/director of media, says of

McCann's hiring practices: "We don't necessarily look for business backgrounds. Some of our more arresting and successful employees have had backgrounds in music . . . music majors, English majors, business majors. We're rather eclectic. Promotions come faster than at other agencies. Most of the people at the top levels have been there at least seven years, some more than twenty."

GREY ADVERTISING

Grey, another giant agency headquartered in New York, with branch offices all over the world, has a twenty-two-session training program to familiarize entry-level people with all departments and functions within the agency and its divisions. Highlights include presentation workshops, business-writing classes, training in listening skills, and advertising-copy education (for account-management people). In addition, there are a general orientation to the agency and visits to the media (TV stations, magazine and newspaper offices, etc.). Other programs include training in the basic media sources (terminology, concepts), discussion sessions that take place during luncheons, and periodic group meetings to discuss research issues.

In the media department at Grey there is a "foster parent" program. Each entry-level person is assigned a senior media person. During the first few months the two meet three times to talk out any problems. As long as the trainee remains at Grey, he or she will have this mentor to consult.

LEO BURNETT COMPANY

This Chicago-based agency has total U.S. billings of over $2 billion. It is listed in the book by Levering, Moskowitz, and Katz, *The 100 Best Companies to Work for in America*. Small wonder. Burnett has a super benefits package, including a contribution of 15 percent of every employee's salary and bonus to his profit-sharing plan. The agency also pays new recruits 50 percent more than the norm for most agencies, including those in New York.

All Burnett media department recruits, as well as about a third of their client-services recruits, start as planner/buyers in the media department. There they are put through a rigorous training program that includes class lectures in media research and evening seminars on a variety of topics, from sales promotion to legal issues. Trainees are given a formal review every four to six months. Planner/buyers generally rise to the position of media supervisor in about two years. About 40 percent of Burnett's media-department recruits reach the level of media supervisor.

Leo Burnett's production-department training program is even more intense. It runs for three to five years. When the trainees graduate, they are considered to be qualified as producers. In the first year of training, a production trainee spends a great deal of time in the agency's video transfer facility. Here he or she learns to edit such unglamorous stuff as sales films. Also on the first-year agenda are courses on the music business, focusing on negotiations, costs, and new recording developments.

The big test of year one is the first production shoot. During this year all trainees are required to go on one working trip where they make major contributions under the watchful eye of a senior-level producer.

In the second year, they start to bid jobs and estimate real ongoing projects. Beyond year two, the work load increases even more—more decisions, estimates, preproduction meetings, shoots, editing, etc. The final evaluation is based on the quality of a trainee's work in all these activities.

YOUNG & RUBICAM USA

Young & Rubicam (Y&R) concentrates its recruiting on four or five of the top graduate schools of business. The agency's objective in its training program is preparing these elite graduates for leadership roles.

Account management is the focus of Y&R's program. A new employee must first earn his stripes as a traffic coordinator for about a year before he is promoted to assistant account executive and assigned to an account group. While on this assignment he is learning by doing, attending in-house meetings, visiting clients, etc. Every six months he is rotated to a different account group so that he varies his experience. The advertising needs of TWA, for example, are far removed from those of Jell-O. The in-training assistant account executive sees both sides.

While on this account group, the assistant account executive is also dealing with the media and creative divisions of the agency assigned to his account group. An essential part of this on-the-job training are seminars and workshops, with role-playing and case studies conducted by agency heavyweights. The trainee must attend these for at least two hours a week for at least nine months. He or she is also assigned a mentor from within the agency who acts as a personal tutor and monitors the trainee's progress.

The media and creative departments of the agency have their own training programs, as do the domestic and foreign branch offices.

In media, the training program lasts for thirty-two weeks, taking up two hours at lunchtime every Wednesday. One recent class was sixty strong. Trainees work while they study. Advancement comes fast.

D'ARCY MASIUS BENTON & BOWLES

Headquartered in St. Louis, D'Arcy Masius Benton & Bowles (DMB&B) is another worldwide agency group with a strong training program for all new media-department employees. It has been in existence for over ten years. The thirty-two in-depth sessions cover an overview of the media function, broadcast, print, and media planning. Included in these sessions are tours to TV stations and the offices of magazines.

One advertising media veteran, Mike Drexler, thinks that agency training should not be specialized into one area such as media but should cover every area of advertising—account management, media, and creative.

Yet critics doubt that training is necessary for everyone. "Advertising majors, for instance, can prosper on the basic knowledge received in college," contends Kurt Wildermuth, assistant professor of advertising at the University of Missouri. We are inclined to disagree. Judging from the training programs we've seen, they are a major advantage in career development.

In the next part of this book we interview advertising people for their perspective on the ad business.

PART V

From the Horse's Mouth: Interviews with Advertising Pros

CHAPTER 22

Sage Advice from an Ad-Industry Veteran

Bill Pitts, former vice chairman and marketing and research director Lois/GGK New York, is an accomplished marketing professional with unmatched experience in promotion, market research, and merchandising. Merchandising is a broad term relating to the presentation of a product to the right market by carrying out such programs as displays or couponing. He began his advertising career in the early 1950s and has spent more than thirty-five years in this field.

Over the years he has been marketing strategist on major ad campaigns for Olivetti, Honda, Sheraton, Qwip, Arby's Fast Food, Dictaphone, and the Dreyfus Corporation. He created and edited the prestigious Dreyfus newsletter "Letter from the Lion."

Many young people, seduced by the supposed glamour of Madison Avenue, are drawn to agencies right after college. What path would you chart for a bright young liberal arts graduate determined to make it to the top in ten years?

The advertising business offers several sectors for career advancement: creative, account management, media. If the bright young liberal arts graduate is determined to make it to the top in ten years, he should first become professionally trained in media and/or account management. The best way to obtain this experience is through the training that certain large agencies like Ogilvy & Mather Worldwide offer to a limited number of applicants.

If the new graduate is interested in creative work, a good sample book of hypothetical ads for well-known advertising brands is absolutely essential. Astute creative directors study these books and can spot high potential talent. My partner, George Lois, our agency's chairman and creative director, can spot a spunky headline, flip through three more pages, and come away with an exact fix on that person's creative possibilities.

But whether the path is through media, account management, marketing, or creative, anyone who wants to make it to the top in ten years has to risk himself in the classic entrepreneurial style: Get some basic experience. If you are fortunate enough to be at the heart of at least one famous campaign, you're on your way.

We know that there are pros and cons to each, but do you recommend a small or a large agency as the best training ground?

Large agencies do offer newcomers professional training, and that's an invaluable way to start. But after the training, many big-agency people can end up feeling pigeonholed or stymied or unrecognized.

By contrast, the smaller agency is usually personnel-shy and calls on its people to go beyond their job descriptions. The learning process here can be accelerated, but the disciplines that should accompany the learning are lacking.

Ultimately, it comes down to personality. If you're spontaneous, resourceful, loose, and very smart, you can probably cut the mustard in a large or small shop. If you require more structure, if you're uncomfortable in working without moorings, you'll be miserable in a small shop but not necessarily a whiz in a big agency. It may be that you should not be in advertising at all—it's a profession that places intense demands on every aspect of your mind and heart. Therefore, if you *know* you're terrific, plunge in, work hard, speak up, and do your damnedest every day.

Although there are ad agencies in all fifty states, they predominate in New York, Chicago, and Los Angeles. Is there exceptional advertising produced in smaller cities, and are the salary levels substantially lower outside major metropolitan areas?

Of course, there are many superb campaigns created in smaller cities. Boston, Washington, Dallas, Detroit, Pittsburgh, and San Francisco would probably fit the definition.

If you start out working in a small-city shop, if you love the work and commute to your office in less than a half hour, you may have everything that so many urban-shocked people are lusting for. If you can move up to an equity position, that's even closer to nirvana. On the other hand, despite the outward advantages of working in a smaller city, such as the lower cost of living, you probably earn less than in a major town, and your chances for a job switch are probably quite limited.

Go through the *Standard Directory of Advertising Agencies* and count the agencies in the cities I've mentioned. Then go through the shops located in New York and you'll get the picture.

Who are the real elite in an ad agency—the creative, account, or media people?

The agency's elite are its creative people. Ultimately, after all the marketing analyses and research findings, copywriters and art directors must create the advertising that does the job. Simultaneously, account people, who have a strong, trusting relationship with the agency's clients and can communicate effectively with the agency's creative group, are surely the agency's elite as well.

Is there a quick way to break into the ad agency business?

I am not being facetious in making the following suggestions:

If you're starting out, you may want to look for a job as a secretary in an ad agency. The turnover is high, and the quality is generally lackluster. A smart, nimble secretary, male or female, is quickly noticed and appreciated. When this happens, it is remarkably easy to move into account work or media buying. Creative is another story—poets don't usually get discovered as secretaries, and they are probably lousy typists.

Are there as many opportunities on the client side of marketing and advertising as there are on the agency side?

I don't have statistics to support my answer, but I have the impression that these days the client side offers a wider range of opportunities. American industry, in increasing numbers of categories, is becoming highly advertising-dependent, while more and more companies are being managed by marketing professionals. By contrast, the ad-agency world is steadily trimming its payroll fat so that the ratio of employees to billings is shrinking. This retrenchment has been further abetted by the mega-merger trend among America's largest agencies, which account for a high percentage of total jobs.

I've seen too many young people sending out earnestly constructed résumés, determined beyond rational discourse to crack an impenetrable ad-agency wall for an entry-level job, while they may hit earlier pay dirt by hunting for work in publishing, service industries, retailing, entertainment, and those many business categories that reflect the U.S.A. of the nineties: advertising-dependent, marketing-based—and always in need of intelligent, resourceful young people.

In going after a job in advertising, either in an ad agency or on the client side, what advice can you give in preparing a résumé?

Keep it short and make it a model of visual clarity: wide margins, neat typing, few bullets, minimum underlining, and an appropriately modest roster of "achievements." Résumés are usually hard to read: short, to-the-point résumés *may* have a chance of being noticed.

Of perhaps greater importance: If you're sending a cover

letter—and you should—keep it short and human. A one-paragraph letter should do the trick. If you can pack a modicum of charm and wit into this brief message, it will wash far better than those long, tedious tomes that are prepared for young people, at considerable cost, by résumé factories.

Advertising is the art of commercial communications; if you prepare a crowded résumé and send it out with a dense letter, you've begun by making two fundamental mistakes. You can, however, get off on the right foot by making your résumé and cover letter as crisp and inviting as a good ad.

CHAPTER 23

Women's Perspectives

WOMEN IN ADVERTISING

Robin Cooper is the publisher of the highly respected ad-industry publication *ADWEEK Western Advertising News,* where she began her career in 1981 as a salesperson. We talked to her about women's progress in advertising and her thoughts on job seeking.

In ad agencies women are receiving the same number of entry-level jobs as men. Are they moving ahead at the same pace, and do they receive equal pay for the same jobs?

Women are progressing at agencies to middle-management status, and some are becoming agency heads. However, there are few that make it to the hallowed ground of the boards of directors. *ADWEEK*'s most recent salary survey shows that men are definitely paid more than women. This disparity seems to be narrowing.

Where do you think women have made the most progress—account management, media, or creative?

Women seem to have made the most progress in the media and account-management departments of agencies; less so in the creative area. Account management is more male-dominated, although women are no longer relegated to feminine-products accounts. We are now seeing women running some auto accounts, though clients still appear to be more comfortable with men on their accounts.

Women who become agency superstars usually have a creative background.

Comparing the client and agency side of advertising, where do you think the greatest opportunities exist for women?

I believe opportunities exist for women on both sides. In the last few years women have been making greater inroads on the client side, and this will filter down to the agency side as well, particularly in the midsize-to-small agencies.

A tough final question: What one special tip can you offer college people and recent graduates who are eager to pursue advertising careers?

I would encourage college people and recent graduates to become marketing experts. Marketing cuts across all disciplines—account management, media, and even creative. I would also advise young people to lower their initial expectations and be willing to pay their dues without immediate advancement. Advertising is a discipline that must be learned and lived. A balance of humility and self-confidence and a lot of common sense are needed. Communications skills are a key to a newcomer's development. Learn to listen and be patient. Don't ever stop learning and being excited about the business.

LIFE OUTSIDE NEW YORK

Martha Pellington started out in media planning at a giant agency. In only a few years she was involved in integrated communications for a major client, the U.S. Army. In this spot she coordinated the client's advertising, direct marketing, public relations, and sales-promotion activities.

It is also interesting to note that although Pellington moved to a much smaller market than New York, she is still playing the big-league advertising game. Earle Palmer Brown is the twenty-first largest advertising agency, with billings exceeding $400 million.

How has your career path led to your present job?

I have a liberal arts background with a B.A. in economics from the University of Virginia. After I graduated from Virginia in 1984, I accepted a media-planning position at Young & Rubicam, New York. My account assignments were Gulf/Chevron Oil and General Foods (Jell-O pudding). A year later I was promoted to a senior planner on Richardson/Vicks (Oil of Olay) and the U.S. Postal Service (Express Mail Service). A year later, I was assigned to the U.S. Army new business pitch which Y&R won early in 1987.

I was promoted to communications supervisor on the army account, responsible for developing and executing integrated communications plans incorporating various communications disciplines (general advertising, direct marketing, public relations, and sales promotion). I worked closely with Y&R's subsidiary companies: Wunderman, Ricotta and Kline (direct marketing), Burson-Marsteller (public relations), and Cato Johnson (sales promotion).

In the fall of 1988 I left Y&R and moved to Baltimore to get married. In the spring of 1989 I accepted a job as an account planner at Earle Palmer Brown in Bethesda, Maryland, responsible for providing key consumer insight and developing consumer-driven strategies for advertising development. I worked on a variety of accounts such as USAir, Roy Rogers, and SkyTel (SkyPager). I also worked on new business assignments, such as the U.S. Marine Corps and Weight Watchers, International.

After Earle Palmer Brown won the Weight Watchers account in August of 1991, I moved into account management as the account supervisor on Weight Watchers. I was recently promoted to vice president in the spring of 1992.

Women have made quantum leaps in the business world in recent years, particularly in advertising. What kinds of discrimination must a woman face on her climb to the top?

I would agree that women have made quantum leaps in the advertising industry, but we still have a long way to go in terms of obtaining senior management positions. And while discrimination varies by agency, I feel it exists more within the ranks of senior management.

Men definitely dominate the management of most major agencies in this country. It seems as though the silent "old boy network" still prevails at most agencies. As long as the senior management on the client side is dominated by men, major agencies will continue to place men at the top.

While there are some women who hold senior positions at agencies, it never seems to be an easy climb to the top. They've had to "play the game" to achieve success and face the politics involved in climbing to the top . . . sometimes at the expense of alienating other women.

In terms of discrimination, there are more demands that a woman must face on her way to the top. To counter traditional stereotypes, a woman must be smarter, have a stronger presence, and be more confident than a man at her level. However, a double standard exists if a woman is too aggressive. She then risks being labeled a "bitch" who is cold and insensitive.

A woman must also face the double standard about the way she looks. A woman must be attractive in the sense that she must dress impeccably and maintain a socially acceptable figure. She must be "polished" and convey a sense of sophistication.

There is a delicate balance women must strive for in senior

management positions in an effort to gain the respect of their clients, their bosses, and their subordinates.

Are there significant support groups available to women in advertising?

None that I am aware of. I know that there are associations exclusively for women in the Washington area, but I don't know of any that are exclusive to the advertising industry.

Are women as successful on the client side of advertising as they are at the agency level?

While there are women on the client side, most of the senior-level clients with whom I have worked are men. In general, I think women are less successful on the client side, probably due to the political and bureaucratic nature of many large conservative corporations.

When do you think women will achieve parity in advertising in terms of salary and position?

I think women are more than twenty to twenty-five years away from truly achieving parity with men in advertising in terms of salary and position. I believe this can be attributed to two things: the obstacles a woman must face on the climb to the top (discussed above) and the fact that many women today are choosing *not* to climb to the top. Some successful women today are choosing to stay at home or accept part-time positions to spend more time with their children.

Women are currently in an age of "choice" in which it is socially acceptable for them to stay at home or pursue a full-time career. However, women are finding it increasingly difficult to "have it all." Therefore, some women will sacrifice being the vice president when they can have a less demanding job and still have time for their families.

CHAPTER 24

Advertising and TV

Richard Low has been a part of network television since its inception as an advertising medium. His career in television began in 1952 at CBS, where he worked first in the news division and then for the television network. He joined Young & Rubicam in 1962 and in 1973 became head of its broadcast department, where he remained until his retirement in 1985.

Low's activity on behalf of clients covered the gamut from "Specials" with Henry Kissinger and Steve Martin to special events, such as coverage of the Apollo mission, the Tonys, and the Kennedy Center honors. He was a member of the board of governors of the National Academy of Television Arts and Sciences, the National Council on the Arts Media Task Force, a judge of the International Emmys, and an adviser to the League of Women Voters' presidential TV debates.

How did you decide which programs you would buy time in for a particular client?

That, as the saying goes, is the "$64,000 question." First, the whole process is not so arcane or mysterious as some might think. Yes, making judgments about which new programs will be successful requires all of the analysis and all of the experience and instincts that one can bring to bear; and still the failure rate for new programs in prime time is often higher than 60 percent. Certainly, a great many high-priced people at the networks with responsibility for spending millions of dollars felt that almost every one of their selections had a good chance of being a hit.

To begin with, you gather as much information as possible. The first step is to make an assessment of the number of households that use television in the time period the program is scheduled and how that usage varies by the time of the year. You then factor in the rating—percentage of the television universe—of the preceding program, the competition, and to some extent even the program that follows. Obviously, the more that any of these elements involves programming with a track record, the easier it is to estimate the range of the audience that is possible for the new entry. The same process is then used, hopefully, by your research department to give you a demographic breakdown for each program, again using as much of past history as is applicable.

Now you have to decide where the new program will fit inside the potential range for its audience and whether it is so appealing that it will bring new people into the time period and exceed the range or, on the other hand, be so bad that it will fall below the theoretical bottom of the range.

At last, the $64,000 question: How do you decide that? You look at a pilot that a network screens for you. Sometimes the pilot will be in the form of a made-for-television movie, which will be much longer than any episode in the series. In every case, more time and money have been spent on a complete pilot program than will be spent on any episodes in the series. More often than not, it is directed by a premier director who may not work on any series episode.

The key question is whether it will appeal to the large-scale audience of television today. What types of programming seem to be declining in appeal, and what kinds of programming seem to be increasing in appeal? Does the appealing pilot have the ingredients of a successful series? Is there a pilot that is less than successful but has the ingredients of a successful series? And, finally, does your "gut" tell you that this program will be successful?

And so you decide. Now you can begin to understand the enormous difficulty and failure rate, which is not unlike that in movies or theater and wherever creativity and assessing the marketplace are principal elements.

How do you determine which programs should be bought?

Here we begin with the client. What is the marketing strategy or plan for each of the client's brands? Based on the answer, a media plan is put together which covers, among other things, the principal and secondary targets; that is the prospective buyers broken down by sex and age and sometimes by additional factors ranging from income and educational level to psychological/social values—what the budget is, when the advertising is to run, and how many of the potential prospects you want to reach and with what frequency.

The next element is to look at each of the programs and in fact at each of the different dayparts of television [a daypart is a particular segment of a broadcasting day] to see the breakdown of the components within the audience. For example, women are dominant in daytime, sports programming is viewed largely by men, and prime time is a dual-audience vehicle, with a skew toward women.

To carry this one step further, assume that your principal target is women age eighteen to thirty-four and you want the broader reach offered by prime time. You have your own estimates of how well each program will do and how the audience for each one will break down demographically. And the networks have their own estimates. You tell them how much money there is or how much of the budget they can try to obtain and when the advertising has to run; then the negotiations begin. Usually, you want the added reach that is obtainable by having commercial units in a number of programs on at least two of the three networks. Ultimately, the buy is made on the basis of negotiating and buying at the lowest cost per thousand against one's principal prospects.

What is the best career path for someone who aspires to your former agency position?

There is no one way, but if I had to chart an ideal path, it might be the following: First, obtain a job with an agency that offers a media training program; then buy network television for two to four years; then move to a supervisory position either at your first agency or at another one or—probably best of all— get a job selling at one of the networks. From there, you can move to sales management, perhaps to programming, or back to an agency where you might be running the buying operation.

To what extent does the client become involved in purchasing?

There are as many answers to this as there are clients, but essentially there are two kinds of involvement, depending on the type of buying that is being done. An overwhelming number of clients are interested in efficiency, with the right mix of quality and some reach and frequency requirements; they are not interested in sponsorships.

The client's dollars are largely spent in thirty-second announcements and now, increasingly, in fifteen-second announcements in a good number of programs on two or three of the networks. If it's a large advertiser, the buy is generally made for the fifty-two-week period, beginning with the "new season," which starts in mid-September.

Here, if you're doing your job properly, before you begin buying, you let the client know what you think the market will be like in pricing and efficiencies and what your estimates are of the audience and efficiencies for all the new and renewing programs. You also discuss your proposed buying strategies:

how much you think should be put into the fifty-two-week "up-front" marketplace; how much you may wish to hold back for "opportunistic" buying in future quarters; and how you plan to approach the networks. As just one example, if you plan to make a buy on only two of the networks, you might wish to ask all three of them to come up with plans—a list of their programs and the number of announcements in them that they are offering, along with how they are scheduled—for half of the budget, 65 percent of the budget, and 35 percent of the budget. Then you can begin to negotiate and decide ultimately what you want to recommend to the client. Obviously, you are more likely to obtain that approval if you fill the client in as the negotiations proceed.

Are there any departments in an agency that seem to have more opportunities than others?

I think almost every department could lay claim to having many opportunities. One of the pleasures of a career in an advertising agency is that you get exposure to and must learn something about so many different businesses, apart from being at the forefront of helping clients to expand their business in an increasingly competitive marketplace. Ulcers, maybe; excitement for sure.

If you're asking which departments are more likely to be the proving grounds for becoming the president of the agency, the answers are account management and creative, but there are exceptions, including, not too long ago, a graduate of Y&R's broadcast department who went on to become the president of another very large agency.

All of which does not diminish the rewards of working in broadcast buying. You not only get to know something about your clients' businesses but also how the mass public of this democracy thinks and feels, and along the way maybe you learn something about entertainment, news, sports, and, it is hoped, how to function in an ever-changing environment.

CHAPTER 25

Advice on
Interviews and Résumés

V eteran media specialist Roger Bumstead has more than thirty
years of broad-scope background in media and marketing
and, most recently, in executive recruiting. Earlier, Bumstead
served as advertising sales director for the Cableshop, the Consumer's
Channel. For more than fifteen years he was a senior vice president
and director of media services for Interpublic's Tinker Campbell-
Ewald and the Marschalk Company. He held similar media management positions with Kelly-Nason, Inc., Campbell-Mithun, and
MacManus, John & Adams, Inc.

Bumstead has served widely on industry committees for the Amer-
ican Association of Advertising Agencies, the International Radio and
TV Executives Society, the Traffic Audit Bureau, and the Audit
Bureau of Circulation.

*How do you go about getting a job after graduation from college? Do
you go to an employment agency or a recruiting search firm, or do you
do it yourself?*

Your future depends on you and no one else. The competition for entry-level jobs in the glamour industries—and, particularly, good ad agencies—is fierce.

Some employment agencies claim to be able to help get you a "starter" job in the ad business. Don't be fooled. They may be able to get you a job as a secretary if you type or can use a word processor or a job in the accounting department, *but not in any vital function offering a career path.*

Despite what college placement people may tell you or the mass media may depict, you are not living in the "Age of Entitlement"—that's a phrase coined by Ira Carlin, the executive vice president and media director of the McCann-Erickson ad agency. No one owes you a job because you have a degree—even a master's.

How do I get a good job?

First, you start thinking early about what you want to do. Use your college's guidance department as a resource to learn more about the types of careers you want to explore. Decide on a *few* types of jobs or career paths that you'd like—ones that best fit your skills and education and, most importantly, your personality. When I say "early," you should have been thinking this over back in high school. By your junior year in college, you should be on the career-goal track to get what you want. Try to get summer jobs and internships that relate to that goal. The real world is goal oriented, and a summer spent "bumming around Europe" or "surfing in Hawaii" doesn't look good on your résumé.

Be more specific.

You'll get your first job by cold calling, letter writing, and networking.

When you know what you want to do, make a long list of companies that might have those types of jobs. Try to get interviews on your vacation time. Most colleges have long Christmas or midwinter breaks: No one will want to see you pre-

Christmas, but early January is a great time to get in the door, with a prior appointment, of course.

I mentioned "networking." That's talking to people who are already working in the fields you have chosen for a career. They may be alumni. The alumni office usually has a readily available list of who does what and where, and someone in the class of '77 or '37 usually is more than willing to help someone from, say, "the good ol' Orange." I went to Syracuse, and any "Orangeperson" sure gets preferential/deferential treatment from me.

Younger alums—in a class a few years ahead of you and in the field you're interested in—should be searched out. They've done it, and they'll sometimes share knowledge of who hires whom, along with the hows and whys. They also may have roommates or friends who work in other "shops."

What should my résumé be like?

It should sell you. It should clearly state what you bring "to the party." The best entry-level résumé I've ever seen is Christina Sherover's [see page 145]. It's career-specific right down to the exact dates she held any interim employment. It exudes energy and leadership.

A couple of other points: If you have a good grade-point average—better than a 3.0—show it. If you've won any awards for educational excellence or leadership, detail them.

Last, if you know how to use a personal computer, mention it. We're already well into the computer age, and I'm amazed at how often recent graduates neglect to put that know-how on their résumés.

Covering letters should be short. Say just what you want—*an interview.*

How do I get experience interviewing?

If you're lucky, your school has a good placement department, and it should help by setting up some role-playing situations and giving advice. If it doesn't, practice with a parent or a "stern-minded" older friend or sister or brother.

What should I say in an interview?

First, do your homework on the company you are interviewing at—its products or services or clients and its field. Learn to use the library. The *Reader's Guide* will lead you to relevant references in *Forbes, Fortune, Business Week,* or the trade press.

Next, talk about yourself—what you've learned, what you offer, and what you can do for Company X. Above all, be interested, enthusiastic, and alert. You'll probably be asked a "curveball" question or two. When this happens, the best gambit is to restate the question verbally, yourself—this gives you time to think about a careful answer.

Do any of the "glamour fields" offer greater opportunities—among themselves—than another?

Not really. One has to be aware of change and how it may impact your career goals. TV didn't kill radio, but it sure changed it. Cable TV has fractionated the viewing levels for the major networks and their affiliates, but it has literally created thousands of new job opportunities, as have videotape, mini cams, and VCRs.

Right now, the specialist ad agencies—many are subsidiaries of the giants—are doing well, particularly in health care, direct marketing, and sales promotion. Look at the company, or at its clients if it's an ad agency, rather than the industry per se.

Should I try to work for a big firm or a small one?

I'd recommend a big, established company for several reasons. A big company is more likely to have in-house training programs. A big company may offer educational benefits if you want to go for a master's. A big company has disciplines—for example, there is a right and a wrong way to write a report for Procter & Gamble. You'll gain a measure of what's good and what's bad about American big business. Most important, a big company—the higher in the top 100 the better—will be very impressive on your résumé when you go for your next spot.

Working for smaller firms, or entrepreneurial firms, offers

you the opportunity to learn more, do more, and have more fun doing it; however, later on you may be turned down for jobs because your background is too eclectic.

While I "made it," so to speak, as a media director in the ad-agency business, my own career growth and income potential was stunted because I had never worked on a major, high-spending, TV-oriented package-goods brand.

Should I try to get a job in one of the "power centers"—New York or Los Angeles—or should I try to get a job in one of the other top twenty-three "media markets"?

There isn't any yes or no answer to that one. What's happening today and what will happen in the years ahead is quite different from how things were twenty or thirty years ago.

You might not make as much money in the smaller markets, but it will go further. Your life-style will be more pleasant, and you'll have quite a bit less stress. Finding a job, too, may be easier simply because there is less competition, even though there are fewer openings. If you stick it out in the hinterlands and you're successful, you'll be a "power" in that pond before you are forty.

The advertising business is not nearly as concentrated as it once was in New York. One source tells me that around 90 percent of all national advertising was created and placed by New York ad agencies twenty-five years ago; now it is reported to be between 50 and 60 percent.

To put it in perspective, there is an ad agency in Cedar Rapids, Iowa, a freestanding subsidiary of Y&R, that spent more than $70 million for its clients in 1990.

Or look at it another way: There are more than 190 ad agencies of substance in the state of Ohio, and they all aren't in Cleveland, Cincinnati, or Columbus.

Lever Brothers uses one agency in Detroit for a well-known brand. Campbell-Mithun-Esty, in Minneapolis, has been a major shop with very big clients for years, and then there's Fallon McElligott in the same city.

In short, if you're good, *you can make it almost anywhere.*

There is one catch, however. If your lust or your ego dictates that you want to make it in New York or Chicago, Detroit, or L.A.—adland—don't wait until your price is out of line with your experience!

Should I pursue a graduate degree?

You are better off with it than without it. It's almost a must for a career in marketing—the client side, or market research—and it's worth a few bucks more if you're headed in the direction of ad-agency account work. It will be worth more in media services in the future than it is now.

Two practical thoughts, however: First, take a break from schooling. Get a job. Learn what the real world is all about. You'll get more out of getting that M.B.A. And not every M.B.A. means the same thing to potential employers; the perceived reputation of the school and its teaching staff is all-important. And, as I said before, find a beneficent first employer who will contribute to the cost, even if you have to be an indentured servant to that company for a few years.

Anything else?

It's there: the gold. Go for it—but it's only you who can make it happen!

GLOSSARY

AAAA the American Association of Advertising Agencies, a trade association of more than four hundred advertising agencies that have one thousand offices in 165 cities.

account sometimes known as the advertiser; the client of an advertising agency, market-research firm, media-buying service, and so forth.

book a portfolio of a creative person's own work or collaborative work—a must for job interviews.

broadcast media electronic media (as differentiated from print media) that include network and spot radio; and network, spot, and cable television.

collateral promotional items that are not considered "measured media" materials, such as print ads or TV and radio commercials. These include brochures, booklets, or any printed or visual materials used in the sales and marketing process; often prepared by agencies for clients.

comp short for "comprehensive layout"; simulates how a finished ad will look.

creative director the head of a creative group at an advertising agency in charge of copywriters, art directors, and TV commercial producers; a senior management position, highly paid.

demographics a term used to identify the various social and economic characteristics of a group of households or individuals. It refers to such statistics as sex, age, education, race, size of family, and economic levels.

direct response a type of "direct sell" advertising that covers mail order and allied fields; includes 800-number messages on TV and radio, coupon advertising, direct mailings, and anything that brings a "direct response" from prospect to advertiser.

focus group a small group of cross-sectional consumers used to pretest ads, themes, and product concepts and to gauge consumer attitudes toward any product, program, subject, or personality.

house agency an advertising agency that is controlled in full or owned by one advertiser.

insertion order the purchase order sent to a publication or broadcast medium by an advertising agency that contains information relating to an ad, radio, or TV commercial—its size, time, rate, frequency, date, and any other special information.

market share the percentage of sales a particular product or service has in relation to its competitive brands.

marketing plan a comprehensive plan prepared by the advertising agency for its clients that defines these factors: size and demographics of the market to be reached, dollars per household needed to reach it, media to be used, dollars needed for each medium, and anticipated sales of the product.

media plan an adjunct to the marketing plan; recommends media and budget allocations to reach target buyers broken down by demographics and purchase patterns.

point of purchase (POP) refers to both displays (in-store, windows, counters, etc.) and literature prepared by advertiser and agency to increase sales at the store or "point of sale."

print magazines (consumer and business) and newspapers where advertising is placed, as distinguished from broadcast media.

product manager sometimes called brand manager; individual at advertiser who is responsible for a particular product's marketing, promotion, and advertising activities and expenditures.

reach a quantitative determination of how many potential prospects for a particular product can be "reached" by advertising in an area or territory.

residuals an amount of money paid to actors in a TV or radio commercial by advertisers for reuse.

saturation the level of advertising placed in one or many media that achieves total coverage of all prospective consumers for a brand or service.

schedule the complete media list of publications, TV, and radio stations in which the advertiser schedules its advertising, showing exact dates of print and broadcast messages.

sole sponsor an advertiser who buys all commercial announcements on a television or radio program.

storyboard sketches of the sequence action in a TV commercial in comic-strip format; used as a guide by the producers and directors and also for theatrical feature films and TV presentations.

unique selling proposition (USP) the distinctive benefit that advertisers seek to persuade consumers that a particular product or service is superior to its competitors.

voice-over a voice used off-camera in a TV commercial.

RECOMMENDED READING

Bly, Robert. *The Copywriter's Handbook*. New York: Henry Holt & Co., 1990.

Bouvee, Courtland L., and William F. Arens. *Contemporary Advertising*. Homewood, Ill.: Richard D. Irwin, Inc., 1986.

Burton, Philip W. *Advertising Copywriting*. 5th ed. New York: John Wiley & Sons, Inc., 1984.

Caples, John. *Advertising Ideas: A Practical Guide to Methods That Make Advertisements Work*. New York: Garland Publishing Co., 1986.

Clark, Eric. *The Want Makers: Inside the World of Advertising*. New York: Penguin Books, 1990.

Fry, Ronald W., ed. *Advertising Career Directory*. 3rd ed. Hawthorne, N.J.: Career Press, Inc., 1988.

Garfunkel, Stanley. *Developing the Advertising Plan: A Practical Guide*. New York: Random House, 1980.

Greenberg, Jan. *Advertising Careers: How Advertising Works and the People Who Make It Happen*. New York: Henry Holt & Co., 1987.

Groome, Harry C., Jr. *Opportunities in Advertising Careers*. Louisville, Ky.: Vocational Guidance Manuals, 1984.

Holme, Bryan. *Advertising: Reflections of a Century.* New York: Viking, 1982.

Internships: Advertising, Marketing, & Public Relations. Hawthorne, N.J.: Career Press, Inc., 1988.

Kaufman, Louis C. *Essentials of Advertising.* 2nd ed. New York: Harcourt Brace, 1987.

Kirkpatrick, Frank. *How to Get the Right Job in Advertising.* Chicago: Contemporary Books, Inc., 1982.

Levering, Robert, Milton Moskowitz, and Michael Katz. *The One Hundred Best Companies to Work for in America.* Reading, Mass.: Addison Wesley, 1985.

Lewis, Herschell G. *Herschell Gordon Lewis on the Art of Copywriting.* Englewood Cliffs, N.J.: Prentice-Hall, 1988.

Lois, George with Bill Pitts. *What's the Big Idea? How to Win with Outrageous Ideas (That Sell!)* New York: Doubleday, 1991.

Moriarty, Sandra E. *Creative Advertising: Theory & Practice.* Englewood Cliffs, N.J.: Prentice-Hall, 1986.

Musto, Ken. *Breaking into Advertising: Making Your Portfolio Work for You.* Princeton, N.J.: Van Nostrand Reinhold, 1988.

Ogilvy, David. *Ogilvy on Advertising.* New York: Random House, 1985.

Paetro, Maxine. *How to Put Your Book Together and Get a Job in Advertising.* New York: E. P. Dutton, 1980.

Pattis, William S. *Opportunities in Advertising Careers.* Lincolnwood, Ill.: VGM Career Horizons, 1984.

Principles of Advertising. New York: Garland Publishing Co., 1985.

Wasserman, Dick. *How to Get Your First Copywriting Job.* Center for Advancement of Advertising, 1986.

White, Roderick. *Advertising: What It Is and How To Do It.* New York: McGraw-Hill, 1981.

INDEX